TAVERNA
by the SEA

One Greek Island Summer

T0053981

Jennifer Barclay

Bradt GUICES

First published in the UK in September 2022 by
Bradt Guides Ltd
31a High Street, Chesham, HP5 1BW, England
www.bradtguides.com

Print edition published in the USA by The Globe Pequot Press Inc,
PO Box 480, Guilford, Connecticut 06437-0480

Text copyright © 2022 Jennifer Barclay
Edited by Samantha Cook
Cover design by Naomi Ann Clarke (w naomiannclarke.co.uk)
Layout and typesetting by Ian Spick (Bradt Guides)
Production managed by Sue Cooper (Bradt Guides) & Page Bros Ltd

ISBN: 9781784779481

British Library Cataloguing in Publication Data
A catalogue record for this book is available from the British Library

Digital conversion by Dataworks
Printed in the UK

ABOUT THE AUTHOR

Jennifer Barclay is the author of *Meeting Mr Kim, Falling in Honey, An Octopus in my Ouzo* and *Wild Abandon*. She also wrote *A Literary Feast* and has edited several collections of literary travel stories. Her writing has featured in a diverse range of major newspapers and magazines including *The Guardian, The Times, The Telegraph,* the *Daily Mail,* the *Mail on Sunday You* magazine, *Metro, Food and Travel, Wanderlust, Psychologies, Woman and Home* and *South China Morning Post,* as well as airline magazines and websites. Her books have been translated into Bulgarian, Latvian, Polish and Turkish, and published in the US and Australia; she has talked about Korean food on Korean television and on BBC Radio 4. She has lived on a Greek island for more than ten years and she writes a blog at w octopus-in-my-ouzo.blogspot.com.

ACKNOWLEDGEMENTS

The biggest thanks as always go to my parents and brother for love and support.

Thanks also to all the team at Bradt for the kind words about the manuscript – just what a writer needs to hear; for giving me a chance to get the story out there, for the opportunity to have Sam Cook's fine editorial expertise once again, and for creating a wonderful cover with Naomi Ann Clarke.

I am grateful to Minas Drakos for encouraging me to tell this story; to Stavros Flouris for being a gentle and reassuring first reader and for input; to Rich Davies for useful feedback; and to Ian Smith.

So many people contributed to my experiences – the community of Olympos, the visitors to the taverna: thank you. I wouldn't have had a story without you.

Finally, thank you to my readers for your support and heartening messages; you make it possible for me to keep doing what I love.

NOTES ON GREEK LANGUAGE

In this book I have generally spelled Greek words as they sound. The location of the taverna is usually spelled Agios (Saint) Minas, but because it's more of a soft 'g' I find 'Ayios' is closer to the correct pronunciation. With the name Minas, the emphasis is on the second syllable, i.e. Mi-nass, not Mee-nas. The name of the village Olympos is pronounced O-lim-boss, with the stress on the first syllable.

CONTENTS

PROLOGUE

I wake up in a panic: there's a large fish in the tent with me. Not alive, but on a platter, and customers outside waiting for it. I sit up, anxious. It's very dark. I can't hear anyone. I realise I must have been dreaming again. It's happening a lot, dreaming that I've forgotten an order during this busiest part of summer.

It felt like a dream, so much of the time: living at a taverna by a beach far from anywhere, on a Greek island. It was a summer of waking to a pink dawn over the olive grove, swimming in moonlight, hearing only the waves or the wind; a kitchen full of creamy yoghurt and honey and tomatoes, olive oil and rosemary and fresh fish. There were days of music; days of no water; days with a goat tied to a tree.

'Must be comfortable in beachwear,' Minas had said, explaining what he wrote in his ads for waitresses in an attempt to get applications from attractive women – and sometimes it succeeded, though that summer the only people who came looking for work were Albanian men. It probably seemed too lonely for most people. For a while I wanted to stay forever; yet I ended up leaving in the night with my dog and my backpack and a bag of money. The story started in late April, when I planned a few days of walking on an island I'd never visited before.

THE HOTEL ON THE MOUNTAIN

'*Kalimera* Jennifer!' Irini shouted out, as she did every morning when she walked past my house. It was a lovely ritual.

I was sitting at my desk, where the window looked out over a medieval chapel and to sweeping views of the wild hillsides of the island of Tilos. Lisa, my honey-blonde golden retriever mixed with something slightly smaller and more annoying, was barking through the railings while wagging her tail just as she did whenever Irini or anyone else passed. Living in the middle of a Greek village, it was tricky sometimes having a dog who barked at every footfall or cat. Still, it gave me a good reason to get up and leave off my work at the laptop for a moment. I stepped outside to grab her and calm her down.

'Have you noticed how every morning I say "good day"? What a beautiful day.' Irini sighed and leaned on her stick as she paused to enjoy the view, the light and warmth of spring. 'Does England have sun like this?'

I laughed and said no – it was one of the reasons why I'd moved to Greece five years earlier – as I stood in the courtyard with the lemon tree, remembering I needed to sweep up the fallen leaves before I left for my trip.

'You're up early working and I'm late, I'm lazy!' noted Irini.

'But Irini, do you ever take a day off? I'm going on holiday this week!'

'Ah, that's good, *kori mou*.' She often used this term of endearment, literally 'my daughter'.

As Irini continued on her way to open her little shop, Lisa went immediately back to snoozing in the shade while I reluctantly returned to my desk.

For someone who loved books, reading and writing and working from a little island, my job editing manuscripts from home was perfect. But recently I'd been caught up in an endless project for a client who seemed to be going mad. I desperately wanted to close the computer and not open it for a very long time.

Thankfully, the conclusion was now in sight, the light at the end of the tunnel, and I'd booked myself an open-ended trip to the island of Karpathos. For a writing project of my own, I'd been researching the deserted places of the Dodecanese, the group of islands where I lived, inspired by the people still living in remote areas. I'd recently had a few days wandering alone around the biggest mountain on Rhodes and was excited to do some hikes around a village called Olympos in the north of Karpathos that was celebrated for clinging on to its cultural traditions.

Karpathos wasn't far away; in fact, from the village where I lived, the island was visible on the horizon on clear days. But getting there wasn't straightforward, involving two ferry journeys. I'd originally planned to visit earlier, wanting to witness everyday life outside the tourism season, and had found a hotel online, but was surprised by the distances involved. It was a big island, the third biggest in the Dodecanese, and although it had an airport in the south, there was little public transport to the north in winter. I decided to wait until I had more time and arrange for a pet-sitter for Lisa. While I didn't like leaving her behind, it could be difficult travelling with a dog. Through a pet-sitting website I'd connected with a young American woman called Tess who would come and stay in my house.

When almost ready to leave, I had problems booking a ticket online for the *Prevelis* ferry from Rhodes to Diafani, the port in the north of Karpathos closest to Olympos. 'No availability,' declared the website, which seemed unlikely. I contacted Minas, the hotel owner I'd been emailing in Olympos, who explained that the ferry dock in Diafani had been destroyed by a storm so the ship couldn't land there. I'd have to make the long journey from Pigadia, the port in the south, but the bus only ran once a week, three days after the ferry arrived. The whole thing seemed a bit difficult, but somehow that made it more intriguing. I decided just to set off and see what happened. I hoped to get to Olympos a few days before Easter week, at the end of April, and booked three nights at the hotel.

Tess arrived on the boat and I was reassured by her open, adaptable nature. Tilos was green and lush with gentle weather at this time of year and she seemed very happy to borrow my home and canine companion and get to know my neighbours. I wasn't sure exactly how long I'd be gone, maybe a week, maybe two, depending on ferry connections, but she could do her work from anywhere and was content to stay as long as needed.

I left on the Friday boat to Rhodes, where I finished the project from hell while awaiting my onward ferry connection south. I was relaxed and excited now the journey had begun, pleased to be meeting people and speaking Greek. A local friend of mine commented that Olympos was a difficult place; when I asked her why she just said, 'You will see.' Sipping wine in a bar on Pythagoras Street close to midnight on Saturday, I met a young bartender who presented me with a white rose that he made out of a napkin. The guys at the bar bought me another drink and confirmed it was worth going to Olympos: it was beautiful; they still made traditional leather boots there; and it had always been a matriarchal society, the women inheriting property and being in charge of the money. But there would be nothing to do except eat and sleep, said the bartender, although he'd never been there. 'You must come back here for Easter. If you don't, you're in big trouble.'

Grinning, at 2am I retrieved my backpack with the tent strapped on to it, waved goodbye and walked to the port past crowds of people standing outside the music bars of the Old Town, thinking how much I loved life in Greece.

My first Greek holidays had been as a child with my family, leading to longer trips and a year in Greece after university, but I'd then felt a need to leave to start my career. I spent my twenties in Canada, had a couple of years in France and then in my thirties returned to England, from where I started travelling to Greece again. Finally, a twist or two in life when I was around forty led me to pursue my lifelong dream of living on a Greek island.

I'd learned to trust in the happiness I derived from being in a place that inspired me. This life gave me the pleasures of walking and swimming surrounded by nature, the time to write, the freedom to make the most of every day and not be tied to a desk for too long. And, whenever I liked, I could hop on a ferry to another island for an adventure.

A Greek woman has since taught me an apt expression: Where are you going? *To the unknown, with hope as my boat.*

❖ ❖ ❖ ❖

I woke in my sleeping bag and stepped out on deck to a bright, sunny morning, the ferry engine thrumming noisily. The only land in sight was a fantastical, rugged coastline of mountain ridge rising from deep blue sea, with the occasional village up high.

Full of anticipation, I disembarked at the main town of Karpathos, also known as Pigadia ('Wells'). Having confirmed that there was no bus to the north of the island for days, and preferring not to spend close to a hundred euros on the hour-long taxi ride or renting a car for a few days, I called Minas, the owner of the hotel in Olympos, to say I might not make it that night. He said it was common to hitchhike and, failing that, a friend of his would be driving up the next morning and could give me a ride. I set off in warm spring sunshine to walk around the huge bay and up a winding road into the hills. Exploring on foot was the kind of travel I loved, getting slowly into the quieter hinterland. I'd brought a tent, and although I looked forward to seeing Olympos, a night under the stars was calling.

In the late afternoon, after walking many kilometres, I descended a steep green gorge, leaving a bag with some unnecessary items hanging in a pine tree halfway down. I set up camp on a beach in the empty bay of Ahata, where aquamarine waters lapped the pebbly shore; in the night, the wind became ferocious and I had to move to a more sheltered spot and pile on my clothes, listening to it blowing through the trees as I fell asleep again. Around seven in the morning I woke, packed up and ascended the gorge, picking up the bag I'd left in the tree. I stopped to explore a stone chapel that looked Byzantine, hiked up to a village where, failing to find a café open, I filled my water bottle from a spring and continued on my way. Minas said his friend had been delayed leaving town. Considering this was the main road linking the south with the north of the island, there were surprisingly few vehicles. It was beautiful and peaceful.

I was resting in the shade after an hour's walking when an old man in a flatbed truck offered me a lift. We continued along the narrow road at high speed, and I glimpsed a blur of majestic mountains and dramatically sheer limestone cliffs dotted with dark pine trees falling away to blue sea. The driver pointed out the pale sand beach of Apella below, then stopped for a while to milk his goats, and again to check on his bees, before we came to a halt at the village of Spoa, the start of the north. He offered me coffee at an old-fashioned café-bar with a few tables under the shade of a tree. A white van from the neighbouring island of Kasos was parked there, selling cheese made from sheep and goats' milk, and rich creams such as *dhrilla* and buttery *sitaka*. How could I not be enchanted?

When I checked in with Minas, his friend had not yet left, so I set off again on foot, keeping up my energy with some tasty *graviera* cheese. The further north I went, the emptier and vaster it felt, the more raw and elemental the terrain. A pickup truck took me the final kilometres as the road twisted and turned towards Olympos. The people in the truck told me their family had a restaurant, which they'd be opening for Easter. I caught a first glimpse of houses painted white and pale blue and yellow spilling over one another, jostling for position on the spur of a mountain, rising to the belfry of a church like something in a fairy tale, a large pale sun behind.

I'd called Minas to let him know I was arriving, and when I got out of the truck I found him waiting at a café. Not what I'd imagined from the deep Greek-American voice, he was short and slight, wearing a checked shirt and jeans. Welcoming but somewhat serious, he offered me a coffee and then led me along narrow alleyways and up flights of steps until we approached the large church. When we turned left down more steps, I was almost knocked over backwards, partly by the sight of the sea hundreds of metres below, and partly by the strong wind blowing between the houses built into the steep mountainside.

I followed him to a stone house with red-painted shutters, and down red-painted wooden steps to a small courtyard. He opened the door to a room with a traditional bed, the mattress on a wooden platform, from which a window looked straight out across an expanse of sea. When he left, I stood on the large balcony, watching as in the far distance waves crashed against a ragged coast. The sun was descending towards the sea through hazy cloud. Above, the skeletons of windmills and scrubby green slopes appeared through the mist that was flowing over the mountain.

I showered, then went out to see if I could find a beer and maybe a meal. As I wandered two minutes back up the alley to the tiny square and then up another narrower alley, I encountered one of the older ladies of the village, a smiling woman in her early seventies wearing a heavy black dress, black headscarf and colourful apron. She introduced herself as Archontoula, we talked a little, and then she invited me to make myself at home in a room with wooden tables and a tiny kitchen – a space just big enough for her to move around behind the counter.

I ordered a beer, which came with olives and good sourdough bread. When I ordered another beer and asked if there was anything more to eat, she brought me bean soup and a simple salad of tomato and cucumber and cheese, then returned to plaiting strings out of coloured balls of wool, her headscarf continually slipping down over her forehead. She said I should try to stay for Easter; it was about to start and would last for over a week, but I'd only booked a room for three days and plans were complicated by the lack of public transport back to the ferry. Her husband, tall and chestnut-skinned with a luxuriant moustache, reassured me that they would find me a ride when I needed to leave. I paid the small bill, went back to my room, crawled into my comfortable bed and fell happily into a deep, uninterrupted sleep.

The next day, I explored the layers of the village built into the rock: steps zigzagging at odd angles, wood stacks and outdoor ovens, hand-painted friezes on intricate balconies, terraces descending into the river valley planted with olives and figs and vines, and above, the sheer green-grey rock of a bare mountain. Mesmerised by the beauty of the landscape, I followed a footpath around the wild hillsides. The church bells were ringing as I arrived back at my room and glimpsed myself in the mirror looking rosy-cheeked and windswept. Blissfully, there was no television in the room, the Wi-Fi wasn't working and the phone signal was bad; all unusual in these days of super-connectivity and, for me, perfect for disconnecting from the outside world.

Although I knew Olympos had become a magnet for tourists in summer, I was thrilled to get to know it in this season, while people were going about their daily lives. The village did indeed hold strong to certain traditions: the older women wore traditional village dress as their everyday clothes. There were men who made and played musical instruments from wood and goatskin, and a cobbler who made leather boots. The next day I walked through the rural settlement of Avlona and down to the promontory of Vroukounta where ancient graves were cut out of the rock. It was said that Vroukounta had been conquered by Syrians around AD700, and the people had moved up the mountain to found Olympos. There was nothing around but vestiges of an older world, and a mule on the beach.

I returned to my room exhausted, exhilarated, hoping I could stay a few more days. This place had me under its spell. I tried sending a message to Minas, confident it shouldn't be a problem keeping the room since I'd seen no other visitors around. Then I stuffed my old laptop into my bag and headed to the taverna just off the square where I could pick up the community internet, check my work emails and contact Tess.

Minas was sitting at the bar drinking a Coke. 'Hey. Is everything OK with the room?' he asked.

I told him I loved it.

'The building was my grandfather's house. It was a ruin but I've been restoring it.'

'So how many rooms does the hotel have?' I asked, curious. It had seemed bigger on the website. I knew the stone house built into the mountain had another room upstairs from mine, with its door just off the alleyway.

'At the moment just two,' he said. 'I'm still working on the rooms downstairs from yours. In the meantime, I've been renting another building with two other rooms but I'll have to give that back this year.'

'Hotel' seemed a bit of an exaggeration, I thought. As did the advertised Wi-Fi, but no matter – I was in love with the room, especially the bed with its view out to sea and sky.

Minas's uncle Nick, who was short like him and wore spectacles, owned the taverna where we were sitting, and asked if I'd like a shot of raki and some local olives. I accepted and settled in at the bar.

'So you grew up here?' I asked Minas, encouraging him to talk. His story was exactly the kind I wanted to learn about.

'No, a lot of people left the village for work when times were tough in the seventies and went to America. My parents, my uncle Nick. I grew up in Baltimore, but we came back every summer. We had a house in Piraeus too and when I was sixteen I went to a bar and they served me a beer, and I decided I wanted to stay in Greece.'

He told me he'd trained and worked as a refrigeration engineer in Athens, and then had come to live on the island and work for the municipality. He applied for a loan to rebuild his grandfather's house in the traditional village style with wood and stone, to make it available as tourist accommodation, though it went way over budget and was still unfinished. He held a roll-up cigarette in his mouth as he talked.

'I'm sorry I haven't been here for the last couple of days. I've been working at my taverna at Ayios Minas, getting it ready for summer.' I had no idea where that was, so he commandeered my laptop to show me pictures on the internet. I saw a curving bay with cobalt blue water, overlooked by a white church on a cliff.

'The taverna is just back from the beach in the olive trees. In the summer people camp, we have live music, fresh fish every day. I'm advertising for a waitress at the moment.' He quickly tapped out something on the keyboard and showed me. 'Look: "Must be comfortable in beachwear".' That way he was more likely to get applications from attractive women, he said sheepishly grinning, and I laughed. His irreverence felt surprising.

I told him that for my first couple of summers on Tilos I had helped with my boyfriend's *kantina* bar on the beach, wearing a bikini and shorts to work and jumping into the sea when it got too hot. And I reminisced about the hotel I'd worked at for the summer in Oia, Santorini, many years ago, where I put on my swimsuit every morning to clean rooms overlooking the caldera, then went for a swim every lunchtime. Although I was paid a pittance, I always remembered it as one of the best jobs I ever had.

'You should come back to work here for the summer,' he said.

I laughed again, thinking of all the reasons it was unfeasible, and at the same time thinking dreamily how wonderful it sounded, given what I'd seen of the island so far. 'I'd love to – it looks amazing – but unfortunately these days I have my own work to do. And I have a dog.' I wasn't leaving her again for long.

A couple of years before, on Tilos, my friend Ian had announced he was returning to Australia to look after his mother. We'd known one another for several years but I'd been in another relationship and I believed he was too. We realised we had powerful feelings for one another just as he had to leave. 'I'm not going to Australia,' I said, laughing – then I did, following my heart, because we seemed made for each other and we needed to give it a try. But because it was temporary, I'd had to leave Lisa behind. I'd had Lisa since she was a pup and not only did I miss her, but Ian and I both missed Greece with all its quirks and its wild beauty; the situation was harder than we'd expected. He couldn't foresee when he'd be able to leave. And I couldn't stay. I'd left sad and confused, but Lisa had been waiting for me and I wasn't giving her up again.

'Bring your dog – I love dogs. It can keep the goats away from the olive trees. And you can do your own work when we're not busy. There's a little house nearby that just needs fixing up.'

I said I'd check the place out sometime, not seriously intending to do anything about his suggestion, though part of me knew I wanted to do something like that, to take the summer off and live right by the sea. Maybe we all reach a point in life – or several points in life – where the sensible world of work seems less important than enjoying what else the world has to offer.

Nick poured us all another shot of raki, and found a recording of haunting music made a few years ago using the traditional bagpipe or *tsambouna*. He showed me his small wooden lyra – the Karpathian violin – though he hadn't played for a while and it needed tuning.

'Did you get my message about staying a few more days?' I asked Minas.

'What? No, I don't have signal down at the beach... I didn't know you wanted to stay. In any case your room is booked for some of the Swiss walking group who come for Easter every year. You know Easter's a big thing here?'

I knew it was the most important celebration of the year in Greece in general, but it was especially big in Olympos. The women would don their traditional finery and the week extended beyond Easter Sunday to Lambri Triti, Shining Tuesday, when the icons from the church would be carried around the village and down to the cemetery. I was a little crestfallen but I understood. Maybe I could find another place. I'd got friendly with another café owner, Sophia, who had rooms on the other side of the village. Nick disappeared downstairs to cook something.

'Look,' Minas said quickly, 'my uncle needs help here over Easter. Normally I'd do it but I want to work on my own place, and I need to drive to town to get gas.' There was no petrol station in the north of the island. 'I have a room available in the other building, and you can stay for free if you'll help me out and work here a few hours a day through Easter. Just waitressing, clearing tables, making coffees, easy. You'll get your meals too and he'll pay you, and you'll have most of your day free.'

There was also no bank here in the north, I'd realised, so I was close to running out of cash. I didn't want to be paid but free room and board would help me extend my stay. Being involved in a small way might be just what I needed; it might even be fun. In any case, it would be an experience and I didn't have anything to lose. I told Minas I'd think it over and let him know for sure the following day.

In a little while, Nick reappeared with a bowl of *makarounes* for me, a traditional, handmade pasta the village was known for. He'd prepared it simply with onions fried in olive oil and a generous grating of a local hard cheese.

'Eat, Evgenia!' he said, using the Greek version of my name.

I did, gratefully, and it was delicious – as all the local food had been so far. I had a quick check of my emails, saw I'd missed a few calls, and said goodnight.

'It's a terrible signal – I've got none at all in my room,' I explained to the friend who'd called, who sounded suspicious. How could a village on a big island not have phone signal these days? For me it was a good excuse not to look at my phone very much.

The next day, I told Minas I'd give the work a try. He gave me a swift lesson in how to use the old coffee machine behind the bar of the taverna, and said he'd be back to lend a hand for the first day. I moved into my new room in the other building, up the alleyway, with the same view over the sea.

❖ ❖ ❖ ❖

It was one of the first big days of Easter week when in mid-morning I walked over to Nick's taverna and asked how I could help. Many families from Olympos who lived in other parts of Greece or in the US or Australia returned for Easter, and though fewer were able to travel since the economic crisis, still the village was suddenly getting busy. I'd just finished securing fresh paper cloths on the tables when a large group of well-dressed Greek people came in through the door off the square. They congregated around a terrace table and all ordered cappuccinos.

Where was Minas? I could make frappe (instant coffee frothed in a blender and served on ice) and Greek coffee but had never made cappuccino. I struggled to find things as I thought about what I needed to do, making espresso and frothing milk; each one seemed to take an age. My first attempts should have been thrown away, but Nick didn't want to keep people waiting too long or throw away good coffee.

'Take them out to the people, Evgenia,' he said, and I did, cringing.

Then another group arrived. I took their order, then returned to the bar.

'Nick, do you know how to make a latte?'

'What's that?'

'Ah, it's like a very milky coffee, but don't worry, I'll just say we don't have it…'

'No, no, we can make it!' he insisted.

The woman looked slightly horrified when I put the murky concoction in front of her. More tables filled up. I got used to the espresso machine and the ice machine, handled the Greek coffees, the soft drinks… A few people left or complained, but everyone else was happy enough. We made it through. Then the lunch crowd hit.

I smiled and laughed with a cheerful group of middle-aged Greek-American women, took their order and headed back into the bar. Nick, downstairs in the kitchen, had told me to put orders in the dumb waiter – the cupboard in the corner that worked as a lift to take plates up- and downstairs – pressing a button to summon it and then placing the paper inside and sending it down.

I heard the dumb waiter noisily descending. While I was out in the restaurant taking another order, Nick came upstairs. I asked him if he had received the order.

'What order? You have to shout to tell me!'

Oh…

He went downstairs and found the order. I opened the door to check.

'Evgenia!' came the shout through the lift shaft. 'You have to write more big! I can't read this! Big letters!'

I wrote it again in big letters, sent down the dumb waiter again and shouted.

'Evgenia! We don' have that. Ask the customers if they would like something else.'

So I went out to the people who by now were quite hungry, and told the lady that I was so sorry but we didn't have any more aubergine salad. She chose something else and I wrote it in BIG LETTERS and sent it down on the dumb waiter.

'Evgenia! We don' have that neither. They wan' *makarounes*?'

By the time the messages had gone back and forth, the rest of the table had finished their food and the lady with nothing to eat wasn't very happy. Meanwhile I avoided the eyes of the people whose Greek coffee I had forgotten to make, dashed inside into the tiny space behind the bar to discreetly make it, and wondered if I was really cut out for this after all.

I was still hunting around to find things as people started arriving for afternoon drinks. Nick gave me a shot of ouzo, though, and we laughed and everything felt OK. I was halfway through washing a mound of glasses when Minas finally arrived.

'Where were you?!' I asked him. 'Were you late on purpose, to see if I could cope? Anyway, we managed.'

He seemed to try to hide a smile as he lit a cigarette and effortlessly made himself a freddo espresso.

The next day, I considered what I should do. I had an offer of a ride to the ferry with a couple of other travellers in a couple of days – a dozen or so more foreigners had arrived for Easter – but I decided I could make it through the week; however inept my help seemed, it was better than nothing.

I went to work, making coffees, serving lunches, watching people come and go for the celebrations in the church; then walking the hills for hours before returning in the evening, when often the work involved little more than chatting with people. When Nick asked me to sit and keep the local men company while they discussed the slaughtering of goats for the Easter Sunday feast, I felt privileged to be gaining insights into the living traditions.

I liked getting a glimpse of how this time of year felt for the business owners, and feeling somehow useful. There's something about life on a small island that demands resourcefulness and adaptability. My ex-boyfriend on Tilos had worked as a plumber and electrician and as a fisherman and then bought a beach bar and had run that too – the one I'd helped with. Many people do extra work in the summer when the islands are busy with visitors, helping out with a family shop or local restaurant even if they're in a completely different trade, a teacher or a truck driver.

Still, when Nick started talking about me staying for the summer, I vacillated between crazily happy and terrified at what I might be getting myself into. Staying at the beach for the summer, as Minas had suggested, was something quite different from this. As Easter Week drew to a close and many visitors trickled away, the weather turned cold around the village; as evening fell, it grew even colder, the wind blowing through the restaurant, and there wasn't much business. All night, the gusts rattled the windows of my room, and rain seeped in under the door.

Next morning, as I worked at my computer, the sky brightened, the sun came out and everything looked beautiful. I went to Nick's and he was grumpy. When he started talking about me getting my hair cut and wearing more waitress-y clothes, I knew I couldn't do this any longer. I took a deep breath and told him I had to leave.

I sent Minas a message, then with a huge sense of relief I shook my long hair out of its pony tail, changed into my shorts and walking boots and hit the road.

THE TAVERNA
AT THE BEACH

The valleys around Olympos were lush and green, and once I reached the ridge, the land descended in tapering fingers towards the blue sea. I was free again – walking along the road for hours, with sea and hills and nothing else – as I headed to see Minas's taverna at the beach.

I'd never seen a landscape quite as dramatic and empty; the wild north of the island was protected against development. Amid a heady scent of pines, I turned off the road on to a dirt track that wound around hillsides, whose slopes fell away steeply on either side to thick trees. It was so easy to be captivated by an unspoiled Greek island in early May, with the promise of summer in the air.

The track split into two, twisting down on either side into flat valleys filled with olive trees and dotted sporadically with tiny houses. I reached the white church dedicated to Ayios Minas, Saint Minas, after whom many men on the island were named, and looked down at a perfect curve of beach and clear blue sea. Dark grey cliffs covered in deep green mastic bushes enclosed the bay, with goats scaling the sheer scree.

Set back from the beach amid olive groves was a cluster of houses. Minas had told me his place was the closest to the beach. I followed the track past closed-up buildings until I came to what looked like a restaurant terrace strewn with kitchen equipment and surrounded by olive trees. Fridges and furniture were scattered haphazardly, and there was Minas looking more relaxed than I'd seen him before, dressed in old jeans and a Baltimore sweatshirt and a baseball cap covered in dust, plastering over holes in the walls.

'Sorry about the mess,' he said, taking a sip of his frappe. 'I've got some improvements to make before we open up. Want a coffee?'

'It's OK, thanks, I'm fine. I just want to say sorry I had to quit.'

'Don't worry, Evgenia, you helped him through Easter. Go see the beach, relax, swim.'

I walked through a field, past fig trees and more olive trees, heading for a gap in an old dry-stone wall, then stood and looked out across a stretch of pale grey pebbles gleaming in the hazy sunshine. As I took off my shoes, I realised the stones were flat and wonderfully smooth, becoming finer closer to shore, where the water, the clearest I'd ever seen, turned them a glossy black. What a magical place to have a taverna, in this isolated bay. There was no-one at all around.

The sea hadn't yet lost its winter chill, so I braced myself for the cool water and dived in, ducking under a few times until my body adjusted and then swam out further towards the empty horizon, exhilarated. Then a white fishing boat appeared around the headland and started gliding into shore. As I swam back to the beach to grab my clothes and get dressed, Minas appeared through the gap in the trees and walked down to the water's edge to help the boat moor. He beckoned me over.

We used a wooden ladder to climb aboard, and he introduced me to the fisherman, Stamatis, a man in his forties with short brown hair, soft features and a kindly expression. They were friends but hadn't seen one another all winter. Stamatis greeted me warmly and, seeing I was shivering, gave me a jacket to put on, asking his assistant to make me hot tea while they packed a big catch of fish on ice. The boat was piled high with coiled yellow nets and baskets and buckets, with a winch and a shade over part of the deck.

'You want to eat fish later?' asked Minas.

It seemed a wonderful idea. Since the only buildings allowed in the valley were agricultural, for people to stay in while harvesting their olives, Minas had rented an old farm building about six years earlier, he explained, and gradually adapted it into a taverna, adding a little each year. He'd dug out a lower floor to extend the ceiling height, and fitted out the kitchen to meet restaurant regulations so he could get a proper licence, as well as putting in a bathroom and laying a terrace for tables and chairs.

I offered to help clean up inside, not anticipating the extent of the chaos. I picked my way over broken glass and upturned equipment and old boxes. It was as if he'd thrown a big party, then closed the door and left everything for several months. A mouse or two had made its home there over the winter, and mould was growing among the dirty dishes and glasses in the sinks.

'I had to work away last year and let my cousin run the place. He left it like this.'

There was hot water and two huge sinks, and it was satisfying transforming the filth and mess into something acceptable. Meanwhile, outside the evening was turning too cool for shorts. Minas asked if I'd fit into his clean jeans – he could keep wearing the work ones half-covered in plaster. I'm a little taller than the average, and he was a little shorter, and skinny, but I did fit into his jeans, just, and felt more comfortable.

Stamatis returned at dusk with heaps of little blue-striped fish called *menoula*, which I'd never eaten before – while Minas lit a barbecue and asked if I knew how to make a salad with tomatoes and onions and olives. He brought out clean glasses, ouzo and water. We'd cleared a little space in the corner of the open terrace in the middle of the valley, surrounded by the dark shapes of low hills. Minas put on some music and together he and Stamatis cooked the fish on the grill over charcoal with a little olive oil. We had a simple open-air feast in the empty valley as the stars appeared.

Minas suggested a toast. 'To the new team.'

I laughed and gave him a quizzical look.

'If you decide to come back and help me for the summer,' he said. 'With the taverna here and with the two rooms of the hotel in Olympos.'

Although I was already living on a Greek island, I'd been looking around for a place to live by the sea, perhaps somewhere that Lisa could run around freely. With his reiterated invitation, Minas was offering just that. It would be an adventure and an opportunity to get to know the village better, too. As for Minas – I liked his creativity and drive and practicality, his cleverness and sense of humour; the way he loved his island, recognised it was special and wanted to build something with what he had here, despite the difficulties. We had both lived in Greece and elsewhere, spoke Greek and English, seemed to communicate well. There was some kind of good energy between us, an easy closeness.

When Stamatis returned to the boat to sleep so he could get up in the early hours and head straight out to his nets, Minas and I sat and talked a little longer. He wouldn't open the taverna properly before the end of May: enough time for him to get the place into shape, and for me to go home and prepare if I chose to return. I didn't want a job, I clarified – didn't want to be paid and create tax complications, or make that sort of commitment – but I was drawn by the notion of living here for a summer, learning more about local food and being able to write about it. From my point of view he was offering a doorway into the community; a chance to get under the skin of the place; to stay for a while in an olive-filled valley populated only by goats, by a pristine beach with no development to spoil it, no rooms to rent, no way to stay here otherwise. In return for having all my expenses covered, I would work for free. Naturally, that suited him – especially since he was starting the season with pretty much no money.

Eventually he would fix up the little house nearby for me; I hadn't seen it yet, but he said it belonged to one of the ladies of the village, who allowed him to use it. To start with, though, sleeping in a tent would suit. In the hot days of summer, my house on Tilos was so stuffy that I often slept outside on the terrace under a mosquito net, blocking out the bright streetlight with a rigged-up shelter of sheets. Lisa usually lay all day in the shade until it was cool enough for us to walk to a beach. She would love a summer by the sea too.

Minas was used to sleeping on a bench on the terrace when he stayed at the taverna, so that night he found some mattresses, pillows and sleeping bags, and cleared some space, and we fell asleep there – until we were awoken by raindrops in the middle of the night and had to make a dash for the kitchen.

In the morning, the sun was bright and the valley silent apart from the breeze in the olive trees and the occasional bird singing. Then a truck drove down the track and it was Minas's cousin Evgenia, who kept the goats in the valley. I'd met her in the village; a few years younger than me with dark eyes and curly dark hair, she dressed in tight jeans and had a lovely, warm smile. He gave her some of the fish Stamatis had brought, and she was delighted. And from their farm she'd brought us homemade bread and the thick, pungent sour cream called *dhrilla*.

I was sure living here would teach me a lot. The leap I'd taken when I decided to work from home from a Greek island, followed by the step to becoming completely freelance, meant I could take chances like this. If Minas and I could get along well and help each other, that sounded good. Surrounded by such a landscape and culture, I couldn't resist the idea: to live somewhere remote, by the sea, a truly different kind of life for a few months.

❖ ❖ ❖ ❖

Minas offered to drive me to the airport in the far south of the island in two days' time as he had business to do over on the big island of Rhodes, the administrative centre for the southern Dodecanese, and had already booked his flight on the tiny plane for Sunday evening. I was put on the reserve list for the same flight; if I didn't get on, I'd take the next seat available.

Now that I'd got to know him a little better, we talked about more personal things. The house where he was now living was his mother's, though she lived most of the year in Piraeus; his father had died while still young. He was proud of his three sisters, who lived in Piraeus, Dubai and Aberdeen, and was devoted to his oldest nephew. They seemed a close family and there was more to him than met the eye. I liked the picture that was emerging.

But if we seemed to be heading in the direction of becoming something a bit more than friends, we had to remain at a distance in the village, which was still traditional; people had to be careful about what they were seen doing. On Saturday night we had a last drink at Nick's taverna – Nick had forgiven me for quitting, after a word from Minas – and it was close to midnight when we both received messages saying the Sunday evening flight had been cancelled but we'd been rebooked on the one that left early on Sunday morning.

I'd got a confirmed booking – but it meant being up in five hours. I left to pack.

At dawn, the alarm went off and I opened the window to hear the waves far below, and the bells of the sheep on the sheer, rubbly slope. I sent Minas a message checking he was awake, then I packed my last few things and stood by the gate of his house, from where I could hear the machine as he made himself a frappe. A few other people crossed the square, carrying bags. Something set one of the dogs barking, but otherwise there was just early morning peace...

And then panic. Minas emerged to say he had been looking for his identity card, which he needed to get on the flight. He must have left it at the beach, which would add twenty minutes to the journey time. We hurried to the other side of the village, got into his rusty burgundy Lada Niva and flew south along the winding road. Ten minutes later we turned off and started to bump and twist down the steeper but shorter of the two dirt tracks with sheer drops down either side, the rising sun shining in our eyes. I held on tight and reminded myself he'd done this countless times before.

Eventually we took the final switchback and sped to the taverna. As we approached, he parked underneath an olive tree and said, inexplicably, 'OK, there's a small red container of gas in the back, and an ice cream flyer.'

'Sorry?'

'I want you to pour the gas in the tank so we don't run out on the road.'

I looked at him blankly, wondering what an ice cream flyer was and how the two things were connected.

In the back of the car he found a laminated plastic poster used for advertising ice creams, curled it into a funnel then jammed it into the opening of the petrol tank using a screwdriver. Crouched under the branches of the olive tree, I started pouring as he dashed off to find his identity card.

In no time we were away again, roaring up the steep curves of the track, back to the main road, Minas seriously focused on keeping up speed.

I started to laugh quietly to myself, my lips sealed.

He looked at me. 'What?'

'I'm just glad it's not my fault…' I said, giggling.

The morning sun painted the rock in shades of yellow. The narrow road was full of fallen stones and goats were dithering in the way. It felt so long since I'd come this way, walking and hitchhiking, though it was only just over two weeks. We reached the airport car park, and as I grabbed my bag, Minas opened up the bonnet of the car.

'I have to disconnect something in the battery.'

We ran into the little airport, went straight through to board and were soon flying over the island, to touch down in another world.

❖ ❖ ❖ ❖

Lisa, half golden retriever and half kangaroo, leapt up to put her front paws around me as I came through the gate, raced around the lemon tree, launched herself through the front door on to the sofa and then raced back to fall upside down for a belly rub. Then she sidled up to Tess to let her know she hadn't forgotten her.

Immensely grateful to Tess for her kindness and flexibility and interested to get to know her, I asked if she fancied staying a few days longer. We took Lisa for a walk to the castle, stayed up late sharing laughs and secrets over a bottle of wine. It was good to have someone to talk to and she loved the sound of what I'd been doing.

In the morning, staring out of my home office window over the medieval chapel as the sunlight crept over the hillside, I could easily have changed my mind about going back. I'd invested a lot of hard work in building up my freelance business. But it was still only May and I'd be able to do my work from the taverna for now; and many companies slowed down or even closed in the middle of summer. Having my expenses paid might help me work less and choose projects carefully. I cancelled my place on a press trip to the nearby Turkish port of Bodrum. The Karpathos adventure was more important.

My old friend Pavlos, whom I'd got to know so well in my first few years on Tilos when I lived at the 'honey factory' house, had died while I was away. Although I knew he'd had cancer, the treatment seemed to have gone well and when I'd seen him, not long before I left for my trip, he'd been joking and laughing. When I'd first arrived on Karpathos and stopped in the village of Spoa, I'd met a relative of his running the café and was looking forward to telling him about it. It didn't seem possible that Pavlos wasn't around any longer, and it was devastating for his family. It put me in a particularly live-life-to-the-full frame of mind. As I'd said when I moved to the island, life is too short not to reach out for what makes you happy.

Home would still be waiting for me, and I'd be taking Lisa. I was trusting my instincts, my heart. A summer lived by the sea felt like something I'd been looking for, and I had to give it a try. I needed to do it for myself.

When I told my neighbour Michaelia about the traditions in Olympos, she sighed and told me how her father had kept sheep and goats and made cheese. It was a way of life that many Greek people already looked on with nostalgia, as something lost.

I hoped to sublet my home for the summer while I was away to cover my rent. My friend Ed, an older English man who'd lived on Tilos for decades, was happy to manage the maintenance of the place in my absence, and I'd pay him for his time. I had dinner with him at the village taverna, Kali Kardia ('Good Heart').

'I'll miss you,' he said. 'Maybe I'll come and visit you there.'

I'd miss Ed too. But I'd only be gone for four months, and I could easily get back here if things went wrong.

I had much to do cleaning and sprucing up the house, as well as my normal work and my tax return and, of course, walking Lisa to one of our favourites beaches every day. My mum was arriving for a holiday, and when I drove down to the port to wait for the late ferry she was on, I lay back in the car and fell asleep.

And then in late May, I was back in Olympos, listening to the sea, the birds, a cockerel. It was bright and sunny, windy and cool, a few clouds coming over. It was all the same, the phone signals haphazard, the internet intermittent, cut off and its own world. Word had got around. People asked, 'Are you working here for the summer? You should! Welcome back…' I felt comfortable and calm with my decision.

Lisa was jumpy about being somewhere new, nervous when other dogs barked, whining and not eating. Everyone started to give me advice – only dry food, only raw food – ignoring the fact that I'd presumably done a reasonable job looking after her so far. Thankfully, she soon settled down. My furry girl was beside herself with excitement as we got into the old Lada and drove to the beach late in the afternoon. I'd bought a pretty cotton bedspread from Rigopoula who had a little sewing workshop and a gift shop in the village, and she said I should leave my dog free in the valley to keep the goats away – she and her husband Yiannis not only had olive trees but also a garden there.

Back in Tilos, I always had to keep Lisa on the rope, away from the roaming goats, as the hunting dog in her overrode her other instincts. One of the farmers had threatened to call the police if he ever saw her off the lead. I wasn't sure if letting her free here was a good idea in the long run, but at least Minas was related to the goat farmers. Allowed her freedom, Lisa raced around with glee and established her territory. Then Minas grabbed a beer for himself and a pork chop bone for Lisa, and spent an hour throwing sticks into the sea for her. He genuinely seemed to enjoy it.

At the beach, the weather was balmy, with none of the cloud and mist of the village. I set up my tent in the field next to the taverna, making it comfortable with a mattress and pillows. There was something wonderful about falling asleep with the stars and moon and waking with the sun, starting the day out in the open with a sense of adventure. Except for the goats, we had the whole magical valley to ourselves, surrounded by fields of olive trees and hills. To get a phone signal, we had to walk up to the clifftop church of Saint Minas, the 'miracle worker'. It was perfect seclusion.

We had electricity and water in the taverna, which was also our kitchen, with an old stove and two big fridges and a freezer, all secondhand and a little worn – Minas was good at fixing things, so he could keep appliances running long after they were thrown out by other people. The taverna terrace was our living room, with plenty of tables and chairs to choose from for my office. The shower was a somewhat makeshift thing behind a cement block wall around the back, with a wooden door and open to the elements. I'd always loved outdoor showers – though this one needed a good cleaning, and a capricious wind would blow your clothes away if they weren't firmly secured.

We would need internet for my work, as well as for managing Airbnb and other bookings for the hotel rooms. With no phone lines in the valley, it would have to be satellite-based. Minas had had it previously but it was now cut off so we needed a new contract and satellite dish. It was hard to arrange without phone signal – the miracle worker could only do so much. It would have to wait. Meanwhile, my old laptop was on its last legs so I had to transfer everything over to the new one I'd brought, but it kept shutting down every time I tried to instal the software. I decided to take a break, luxuriating in the glory of living in a tent in a field at a taverna by the sea with no-one around and no way of being disturbed.

Eventually, we headed back up to the village, driving there together in the Lada. We'd be living at the taverna, but unless we found some help I'd also spend time in Olympos, changing over the hotel rooms for guests. I'd done cleaning work years ago for extra cash while studying at school and university, and then after graduating and moving to Athens to teach English I'd spent the summer working in that hotel in Santorini. It had been an opportunity to spend months for free in one of the most beautiful places in the world, good exercise and no great hardship to spend mornings cleaning rooms with an exceptional view.

We had just two rooms to rent to guests now: the lower room where I'd stayed when I first arrived, and the one above it. Each had a traditional wooden platform bed with a double mattress on the main level and a single mattress on a slightly lower level, divided by wooden posts; each room also had a bathroom and a dining table and chairs;

the upstairs had more windows, an extra bed and two balconies, while the downstairs had a bigger, private terrace with pots of flowers. Minas showed me what needed to be done and where he kept all the cleaning products, soaps and towels and so on, preparing one of the rooms as he did so. Scrubbing the toilet and the shower with bleach, he felt a little embarrassed but I reassured him that cleaning a bathroom was a good look for a man. He wasn't entirely convinced but intrigued and flattered.

Then he drove back to the taverna, leaving me to clean the other room while also catching up on my own work. I enjoyed a proper shower and was preparing to sit at my computer when there was a power cut. Without power, I couldn't do laundry or press sheets either. It was a hot, sunny day, not a cloud in the sky, quiet and beautiful. It seemed the universe was telling me to take another break.

'This is Greece,' said Nikos at Parthenon, the traditional kafencio, or café-bar, on the tiny square below the main church. It seemed most of the men who owned tavernas or bars in the village were called Nikos (Nick). Parthenon, which he ran with his sons and wife Maria, was open all year and was where most men of the village as well as some of the visitors tended to gather. 'Come inside and I'll make you an energy drink, my own recipe with honey and pollen.'

When the power came on, I carried a bundle of sheets over to Minas's house and followed a few flights of steps down to a small, low-ceilinged room with a mound of laundry inside. Both this house and his grandfather's, now the hotel, were built into the side of the mountain, with rooms on several levels. Hotels in towns and cities can send dirty sheets and towels to a laundry service, but that wasn't an option here. Minas's mother usually spent summers at her house here in the village and helped him with the hotel; but she had recently become a grandmother again so she'd be staying in the city.

Ducking under the doorway and setting the machine to run its cycle, I climbed the steps again, walked back to the hotel and descended several flights of steps to pick up the cleaning materials. I dusted the guest room and the carved wooden bed and shelves, disinfected and polished the bathroom, emptied and cleaned the fridge and bins, beat the rugs, and swept and mopped the floor. It was a surprising amount of work.

After that, I walked back across to Minas's house and down the steps to take out the washing and hang it to dry. I carried the wet sheets up to the line in the courtyard, then realised there was nowhere to put the clean laundry down. The table and bench were caked in dust since the house was now sitting empty. Minas had stayed here all winter but probably hadn't used the courtyard much.

I held the precious burden of clean laundry in my arms as I struggled to peg things up one by one on the line, with the wind flipping them around in every direction. A pillowcase fell on the dusty ground; I could use a different one, though it wouldn't match. Then, just as I was finishing and rearranging things so they'd dry nicely, I saw the washing line was caked in dust, too, leaving a black line across the clean linen.

I sighed and took it all back down to the machine, and returned to clean the washing line.

Off the courtyard was a room with an old American steam press and, luckily, a pile of dry laundry that had clearly been sitting there for a while. I'd never used a steam press before. Spritzing the crumpled sheets, I arranged them section by section and closed the press. If left inactive for a few minutes the machine emitted a loud, high-pitched beep, making it impossible to do anything but stand and wait and then slide the hot fabric across the board. Finally, I completed a set of sheets and pillowcases and carried them over to the hotel.

It turned out to be not so easy making up a bed on a wooden platform without creasing the perfect sheets or banging your head on the ceiling. I wondered if fitted sheets might be a good idea. And keeping a supply of spare sheets clean and folded. Pillows fluffed, covers and towels folded, rugs in place, bathroom gleaming; the room built into the rock looked beautiful again, with its view out across an expanse of blue. I walked along the alleyway to the edge of the village to wait for the guests, then walked them to the room, telling them all about Olympos on the way.

When they'd settled in, it felt great to set off walking along the road and to thumb a lift. The older man who stopped to pick me up, a local with an American accent from his years in New York, owned a hotel in Diafani and an excursion boat, and said he'd bring people to the beach at Ayios Minas when he had enough customers. He dropped me off at the track and I walked down, around me a vast panorama of deep blue sea, olive trees and pines. Lisa leapt into my arms. I took her with me straight down to the beach, dived in and swam across the bay, then lay for ages just looking at the sea.

It was still early in the season but the occasional car drove down the road and people might call in for a coffee or a beer. The taverna was now open in a limited way, though while there were few visitors to the beach Minas was still working on improvements, doing structural work to update it inside and out. The terrace was surrounded by low stone walls and covered at one end by a wooden roof for shade. He asked if I wanted to help him put up some more beams across the other side of the terrace so he could extend the roof as soon as he could afford to buy more wood. He'd been given the beams for free; they'd been sitting in a field for a while and looked pretty rotten, but he was sure that once the rest of the wood was in place, the structure would be strong enough. I hoped he was right. I enjoyed helping him; I held the beams while he drilled them in place, then we painted them with dark stain both to protect the wood and improve the look.

The far south of Karpathos, near the airport, was popular with windsurfers. On one rare occasion when there was no wind for surfing in the south, a group of half a dozen guys drove up to the north for the day and dropped in – one of them lived on the island and knew Minas. I helped with the food order and then took Lisa for a walk, leaving the guys to drink beer.

When I returned an hour or so later, Minas was performing his favourite rock ballad by Lynyrd Skynyrd, 'Simple Man', singing along to the karaoke about troubles that would come and would pass, about being true to yourself... Meanwhile, I noticed with dismay, one of the fit young guys was doing pull ups on one of the dodgy new crossbeams. I kept a safe distance and my fingers crossed.

I helped myself to a beer from the fridge and continued to the shore, sat for a while on the beach and listened instead to the waves gently rolling in. When I heard the guys' vehicle drive up the track, I returned to find the roof tested and still intact but bottles and tobacco and plates everywhere. Minas was asleep face-down on the bench and a frying pan with a pancake in it had somehow fallen behind the stove, stuck between it and the wall. Noting from the cash drawer that the guys had left a big tip, I made a salad and poured a glass of wine, brushed my teeth under the stars, happy to be away from village lights, and went to sleep in my tent.

Early next morning, Minas was sitting in the corner of the taverna with a coffee and cigarette and an unexplained injury on his nose.

'Did you punch me?' he asked. 'If you did, I probably deserved it.'

OPEN FOR BUSINESS

It was June and the season had changed abruptly to summer, with consistently hotter weather. The taverna was looking more like a real restaurant, half the terrace cleared and swept with blue-painted tables and chairs neatly arranged and basil plants in the corners, though the other half was still somewhat unfinished, with a broken freezer, an unpainted concrete wall, an ugly mop bucket – and often an array of discarded clothes and shoes belonging to whoever had just gone around the corner to brave the shower. The barbecue was set into a gap in the wooden wall looking towards the beach and the church on the cliffs.

Now that we were open for business, Minas's friend Pavlos visited from time to time in his truck and his snow-white trainers, helping him draw up plans for improvements to the premises or ideas for new projects on scraps of paper in return for lunch and beer. Around our age, Pavlos was a calm, taciturn and respected Albanian man, of average height and sturdily built with dark hair and a nice smile, who'd lived on the island for two decades. His profession was stonework, and he'd built the low walls around the taverna terrace. Minas told me that Pavlos's business slogan was 'Builds with Stone', and that nicely summed him up: straight-up, honest, does what it says on the tin.

Minas had recently decided to paint the exterior of the taverna a deep, rich yellow, a brighter version of the ochre that was traditional in the village. He had asked my opinion before starting and I wasn't sure, but after it was finished, I agreed it looked stunning. Now he asked Pavlos what he thought of the new décor.

'It's too much,' said Pavlos, shaking his head. 'You should have done it less intense.'

It seemed odd to criticise given that it was already completed, but this was a local sort of response. They wouldn't just say something complimentary; they felt the need to say, 'You should have done it like this instead.'

This may be because of the traditional Greek belief that if you praise someone, you're cursing them with the evil eye. Whether I praised him or not, it certainly began to seem as though I had cursed Minas. With construction work ongoing, in the course of a week he dropped his jackhammer on his foot, stepped on a rusty nail with the other foot, and, while making fried potatoes for Pavlos and drinking a beer or three at the same time, sliced a piece of skin almost off his hand using a mandolin in the kitchen. It confirmed my suspicion that the mandolin, with its super-sharp blade, was a dangerous bit of equipment when used with bare hands. Knowing myself to be accident-prone, and knowing how far away the nearest hospital was, I preferred a knife.

Now the tent was baking hot in the mornings, every day I would crawl out in my bikini and walk straight to the beach to jump in the sea. It was such a perfect beach, clean and pure and natural. One day, while Minas was preparing for a trip to town, I took the opportunity to walk Lisa up to the chapel. I looked down at the yellow taverna and my blue tent in the valley and thought how amazing life felt. When I arrived back, I found Minas wearing a pinstriped shirt and a blue towel around his waist while he poured fuel into the car. Heading inside to find our shopping list, I heard him curse and worried he'd injured himself again, but he'd just driven over the broom.

Olympos had only one mini-market and its stock was basic, perhaps because so many people made their own bread and olives and had their own fields. The stock would increase slightly in summer, but most shopping had to be done in Pigadia, otherwise known as Karpathos town, which meant an hour's drive each way. Since arriving back on the island, I'd been to town only once when we'd had a ride with Yiannis the postman in his pickup truck. He'd put Lisa in the flatbed and I'd been terrified to see her standing excitedly with her front paws up on the side-rails as we wove helter-skelter along the winding cliff road. I hadn't found much to occupy me in town and was happy to leave that to Minas. I handed him the list of things we needed – flour and yeast, dog food, washing line... Though with few people around, I'd been hanging any wet washing or my swimsuit to dry in the fig tree.

While Minas was gone, I was in charge of the taverna, and couldn't leave the premises. I did a little cleaning, then measured five cups of flour into one of the five-litre yoghurt containers that were so handy as bowls and buckets. I'd been making bread at home for years, and Minas had showed me how he made a softer dough for rolls. I kneaded a batch, covered it and left it in the sun to rise. Then I made myself a coffee, sat down at a table with my laptop, and did some work. Lisa's barking would alert me when a car or motorbike was approaching down the road. At last, her surprisingly loud barking was coming in useful – and it helped to chase the goats away from people's olives, too. I served a drink or two, and told people what time Minas would be back to cook.

❖ ❖ ❖ ❖

Once, when I was a baby, my mum left me in my pram with the shopping and came back to find me eating a raw potato. That probably says a lot about me: impatient, impulsive, hungry. As I got older, I continued to raid the jars of ingredients in the kitchen cupboards when my parents were out.

My mum co-ran a café and a catering business, and since we lived in a small village, made most of our food from scratch. Her cooking was diverse: stuffed cabbage leaves in yoghurt sauce, fried aubergine and tabbouleh, lamb tagine.

On my dad's side of the family, my Hungarian grandfather, who was an actor and writer in London, published an opinionated cookbook called *The New Gourmet* when I was still a child. His favourite restaurant was Costa's Grill in Notting Hill, which is probably where I first ate Greek food.

I was thirteen when I got my first weekend job helping serve Sunday lunches in a restaurant, learning to wrap cutlery in paper napkins and, as this was in the early eighties in northern England, put little paper doilies around the stems of prawn cocktail glasses. Later I worked on Sundays at McDonald's in a nearby town, wearing a horrible brown polyester uniform and a hairnet; I splatted unpleasantly sweet sauces on to soft, perfectly round buns, polished stainless-steel cabinets when it wasn't busy, and learned that fast food doesn't satisfy me. I gave it up after a month.

A few years afterwards, after my family moved to the south of England, I worked front-of-house at a tiny, exquisite hotel and restaurant, as well as ironing tablecloths, polishing silverware and neatly tucking in bed sheets; I cleaned the kitchen and still remember the smell of that fridge full of creamy desserts. I spent my first summer vacation from university living in a country pub, cycling through green Oxfordshire countryside in between shifts of preparing meals and pouring beer and handling kegs.

With my summers in the Santorini hotel snack bar and island beach bar, learning about Greek food and having lived with a fisherman for a couple of years, I went into this new adventure thinking I knew a thing or two. I was destined – doomed – to help run a Greek fish taverna by the sea.

So when Minas told me I was cutting tomatoes wrongly because I didn't have restaurant experience, I was bemused.

Minas had grown up in his parents' diner in Baltimore. When he was a boy, he pleaded to be allowed to grill a steak; his father told him he would be allowed when he was big enough to be able to reach the grill, so he found a crate to stand on. For years he'd had a good job in Athens working for Coca-Cola as a refrigeration engineer, maintaining cooling systems in bars and big venues, but Minas was never happier than when cooking for someone, and having run his own taverna for six years he had ingrained ways of doing things. What he meant was that there was a way to cut tomatoes that was more efficient when you were busy and also looked good on a plate. There was a particular knife to use and a correct number of slices.

I bristled whenever he criticised – he couldn't boss me around like the young waitresses he was used to hiring. And I didn't always agree. But I also tried to listen. It was his taverna, after all. He knew how to make food look, smell and taste great. And he enjoyed cooking for me. On the same day he found fault with my tomato skills, he made moussaka, brushing the slices of courgette and aubergine and potato with olive oil and cooking them on the griddle. His meat and tomato sauce smelled heavenly, simmered with cinnamon sticks and bay leaves, the dish covered with a smooth, creamy béchamel browned on top.

When an Austrian couple dropped by, decided to stay for dinner and enthused about everything, he rustled up a dessert he'd been experimenting with as a surprise: pancakes and a sauce made with fresh oranges and Metaxa brandy, cinnamon and cloves. Although many things in the kitchen were precisely measured and costed, these creative moments, going the extra mile, were the ones that brought him pleasure.

He also knew how to create a monumental mess in the kitchen. He seemed to prefer it that way: scattered offcuts and implements, mingled juices streaming over the workstation. And in the morning, if he didn't have to drive to town, he'd deep-clean the kitchen with sports radio on and a roll-up cigarette between his lips. It was his therapy, he said.

❖ ❖ ❖ ❖

For several days after Minas sliced his hand with the mandolin, there was still a flap of skin hanging off the palm close to the thumb. He tried covering it up, he tried leaving it exposed, but every now and then it caught on something and was very painful. He couldn't bring himself to cut it off, and I refused to do it for him. One evening we drove up to the village and were having a drink in Parthenon when his relative Vasilis arrived. Vasilis was a thick-set man in a peaked cap with a respectable white moustache and a canny twinkle in his eyes who made goats' cheese and wine and honey at the top of our valley in the cool space beneath a church.

When Minas told him about the flesh hanging off his palm, no-nonsense Vasilis asked to have a look, then whipped out his knife and grabbed Minas's hand – and before anyone could raise an objection, the piece of skin was neatly gone. Minas looked a little green and queasy but a shot of raki soon sorted him out. I listened as he talked to Vasilis about his cheese and honey and asked if we could order a regular supply for the taverna. Ten minutes later Nikos, the café owner, returned from the kitchen and sat down at the table next to the bar where he'd left his drink. We noticed him pick something up off the table next to his glass, thinking it was a peanut, and was about to put it in his mouth when he hesitated and asked, 'What's this?' It was the flap of flesh from Minas's hand.

We giggled about it later as we walked back to the hotel, having decided to stay in the village for the night.

'I want you to help run things with me,' he said, tipsy from the drinks. He talked sometimes about his plans for restoring a windmill he owned, for setting up a taverna elsewhere. He owned various bits of land and had ideas for all sorts of projects and wanted someone to be part of it all – not just a business partner, but someone who wanted to be with him, part of his life. I wondered if it didn't seem such a bad idea; there was certainly something appealing about it. But then again, Minas could be a bit of a handful.

'Thank you for saying that,' I said, genuinely excited by the notion and moved by the suggestion, which I knew he'd repeat sober even though the booze had loosened his tongue tonight. But I still had my doubts. It was too early to respond seriously in any case; I'd like a bit of time to get to know him better. 'Let's see how it goes through the summer, shall we?'

I'd had a bumpy time lately with relationships. The urge to try for a family had come to me late and, before leaving England, I'd got involved with a man who turned out to have lied to me about all sorts of things, including his ability to have children. After that false start, when I moved to Tilos I met someone new, who was honest and good and fun; but being in my early forties already, I had a few failed pregnancies and felt that although we'd have made a good family, we weren't a great couple. Then there was the Australian episode, wonderful while it lasted, and a somewhat confused time since…

All of this put the notion of romance firmly in its place. Although I remained optimistic that one day I'd find myself with the right person, for now I was more interested in being good to myself, and following my instincts in choosing the kind of life that made me happy.

The next morning, as we drove back down to the beach and the battered Lada negotiated the narrow, rough, switchback track with its sheer drops either side, I thought to myself about risks that pay off. There would be twists and turns in life and sometimes things would look scary along the way. Leaving behind my house to live in a tent at this middle-of-nowhere beach had been a gamble, but I had to trust myself, and so far I was being amply rewarded. Sometimes you have to take risks on the road to where you want to be. And for a fairly cautious person, I'd taken a lot of risks, when I thought about it. I'd given up a lot of jobs and homes over the years in different countries; given things my all, then escaped to grasp another opportunity to make the most of life.

The Lada was a 4X4 with a bent front fender, its burgundy paint liberally polka-dotted with rust, which apparently happens to vehicles that live by the sea unless they're washed regularly. The insides were rusted up too, unfortunately not helped by the fact that several bottles of engine oil had apparently been spilled behind the seats, and various sections were missing. The rear door was held up by using a stick wedged in position when we had to load or unload the car. It felt like a rugged island vehicle – my kind of vehicle – and the time had come for me to learn to drive it.

I'd been driving Greek island-style for a few years already, sharing a car with missing wing mirrors and only one working door. While house-sitting on remote smallholdings during that year in Australia I'd got accustomed to driving tank-like utility vehicles – all good practice, yet I was still scared, partly because the road up from the valley left little room for error. I had to pick the right moment, with no-one watching and when I was clear-headed. And one afternoon when I was feeling relaxed, I got in and drove up to the church and down again without incident.

It was absolutely fine, I reported back, except for the fact that the front seat was stuck very far forward, since Minas was shorter than me, and I couldn't budge it back, making it dangerously difficult for my longer legs to manoeuvre the brakes and accelerator. Minas said he'd fix it so I could drive up to the village on my own. In the meantime, we tied a rope to the Lada and used it to pull a big fridge out from the terrace to open up more space.

I walked down to the beach, watched the mauve evening sky over a calm, pale blue sea, and realised how much fun this could be. When visitors had a good time and there was just enough money coming in to keep things ticking over, it felt like making new friends and looking after them at your own home. We still had the valley to ourselves, and mornings and evenings were idyllic and quiet.

But that was about to change, with the arrival of Scooter.

❖ ❖ ❖ ❖

Scooter, in fact pronounced more like Sknterr, was a stocky Albanian man with grey hair and a lopsided grin who'd done casual labour on the island for years. When he turned up at the taverna one day, Minas greeted him like a long-lost friend and hired him right away, even though we had hardly any business yet. Scooter would do the menial stuff like washing dishes and mopping floors, leaving Minas more time to roll cigarettes and worry about money. I wasn't sure that was wise.

It took neither of us long to realise that we had lost our private idyll. At home, I was used to having my own space – my own kitchen and bathroom and office. At the taverna I often did my editorial work at one of the tables during the day until a customer arrived, so it was distracting to have an extra person around. And unfortunately, Scooter liked an audience. Our quiet times would soon be filled with a soundtrack of 'The 100 Best Things about Albania'. I'd have to get used to it.

In any case, since there were a few more potential customers coming down to the beach on these blissful early summer days, Minas often turned the music up to let them know we were open, which made it impossible for me to focus on any text I might be reading. He had speakers rigged up in the corners of the taverna, with a stereo balanced precariously on a shelf by the door. If someone arrived even for a couple of coffees, which Minas could very easily handle on his own, I had nowhere to escape to except the tent, which was in full view of the taverna and very hot. I wished the *spitaki*, the little house just behind the taverna, was useable as an office. Although Minas had promised to clear it out while I was back on Tilos, just as he'd promised internet, it was still piled full of stuff and had mice living in it.

We'd figure things out. Jumping in that clear blue bay every day made it feel worth going with the flow.

Minas put up a new cabinet in the kitchen for glassware, another improvement. He asked me to taste a new topping he'd made for pancakes using fresh strawberries – delicious. For dinner we had a meze of fried aubergines with a homemade tomato sauce, and lamb chops done on the barbecue with a grilled skewer of mushrooms and peppers and courgette, and thick-cut chips. He made great food. And he made me laugh.

'You're my inspiration, *moro mou*,' he said, meaning 'babe'.

Now that I could handle the Lada, I was able to go to the village on my own in the mornings to clean rooms and meet new guests, and with Scooter around to help at the taverna, at least the timing was less fraught. He could help Minas with the preparation, and I didn't have to race back down to help with lunch. Taking our rubbish bags with me, since we had no rubbish collection at the beach, I drove up carefully and calmly, happy with my new freedom. Arriving at the car park at the entrance to the village, I propped the back door of the rusty Lada open with the stick and threw the black bags down into the open bins as the locals did, then parked and walked up the main alleyway, saying hello to everyone.

Shops had opened for the summer tourism season, giving the village a different feel, their wares on display all along the alleyway – leather shoes, lacework, soap, paintings, olivewood, honey. Proprietors stood outside restaurants encouraging visitors to come in, and windows were open into kitchens, displaying tantalising arrays of vegetables and baked dishes. Most visitors came to Olympos by tour bus or rental car for just a few hours in the middle of the day, and locals competed for their attention.

'How are you? How is Minas?' the shop and café owners asked me. 'Have you opened yet? Are there any customers?'

'A few,' I replied. Too much business and people would be jealous, none at all and they'd repeat that Minas was mad for having a taverna in such a remote place. Running a taverna or a restaurant anywhere was a very tricky game, but especially at such an out-of-the-way beach.

Passing Yiannis the postman's souvlaki restaurant, an open window revealing mouth-watering food, I paused to flick through the letters in the box outside to see if there was anything for Minas. Yiannis was a gruff-looking man with a grizzly beard and spectacles who, in between looking after his goats and crops and running his restaurant, was responsible for bringing the post up to the village, where he left it in this box. The only problem was that many people didn't live in the village year-round, and nobody was in a hurry to pick up bills, therefore the box usually contained several hundred envelopes.

I waved to Archontoula, said hello to a few more people and then crossed the square to the other side of the village where the houses clung to the side of the mountain overlooking the sea. I opened up the rooms and bundled up the sheets and towels that needed washing and carried them across to Minas's house, carefully descending the steps that were covered in heaps of bougainvillaea petals and other debris that got blown around by the wild winds. I found the key to the laundry room and ducked my head under the low doorway to load the machine, then set off to start the cleaning. We had a last-minute booking for a Greek family of four who said they'd be arriving at lunchtime, so I hurried to prepare three beds in the upstairs room. Just as I was wondering where they were, we had a call saying they couldn't find us.

'Go to the main church.'

'We're at the main church. Standing outside it.'

'So am I! I should be able to see you.'

After some discussion back and forth, it turned out they'd mixed up the place with another village of the same name at the other end of the country. A place within driving distance of their home. Sigh.

The damp clouds that swept over the mountain and topped up its water supply often covered the village in mist, and today was no exception. The washing wouldn't dry, and I couldn't go back to the beach with the sheets still hanging on the line. I called Minas, and as he and Scooter were busy at the taverna doing outdoor woodwork and praying for customers, we agreed I should stay in the village for the night, where I could relax and catch up on some of my business emails. Both hotel rooms were free, thanks to the booking mix-up.

'If you have time,' he said, 'could you clear out the storeroom? And do your work in the upstairs room at the hotel with the door open, in case anyone's looking for a place. Oh, and can you water the plants at my mom's house?'

So much for a bit of time to myself.

The storeroom was a disaster, but it would be useful to have space to organise things better. 'I'm not really the organising type,' Minas had said, something of an understatement. Later in the day, watering the plants at his house as requested, I found another disaster area: the bathroom he'd been using all winter. It would be nice to be able to use it, but it would need a thorough blitzing and scouring. As I picked up mildewed clothes and emptied the bin, I wondered how he could leave a place in such a state, and then I wondered why I was happy to clean it up.

Sitting in the vacant hotel room with the door ajar and my laptop open on the wooden table, I smiled when visitors passing on their way through the village stopped to remark that the hotel was beautiful. Many of them asked if they could take a photo from the balcony, but nobody was looking for accommodation. It was a wonderful place to work, with the view of blue sea far below. In the quiet of evening, I relaxed on the balcony with a drink. A soft yellow sunset light suffused the white, ochre and blue houses and the old windmills, cloud still sweeping over the top of the mountain, waves lashing the rocky coast far in the distance. Dogs played and sheep roamed on the sheer slope below me.

Later, I walked up to Parthenon café on the little square, taking my laptop with me. Nikos offered me one of his excellent *sardeles*, small fish preserved in salt and olive oil, and I ordered a Greek salad and responded to a personal email or two while listening in to the conversations around me. Yiannis the bootmaker let me know that the villagers would start threshing and winnowing at Avlona soon.

In the morning I watched as the cloud dispersed to leave everything sparkling in the sun. One of the village ladies, a widow in black named Kalliopi, made me a Greek coffee at her tiny café on the square and was happy to have company. Her husband, who had died only the previous year, had been a renowned musician; the walls were covered with photographs of him and other men with musical instruments crowded around the tables here in years gone by. I soaked up the history of the village then sat for a while, trying to reinstal versions of Word on my infuriating laptop using the community internet. Maroukla came by with cherry tomatoes from the pots in her yard, and gave some to me to nibble on as I chatted to Microsoft.

Eventually I called Minas and asked if he needed anything before I drove back to the beach.

'Just get down here,' he said. 'We've got three big tables, some of them old customers from previous years.' He admitted Scooter's constant presence had been driving him mad, and it would be good to have me back.

When I got there, the rush of business was clearly over. The customers had left, Minas was in the hammock with a coffee, and Scooter was sitting bored. But the boys had not been idle; they had covered the pergola over the terrace with cream-coloured canvas to provide shade for the hottest part of the day, which was when we welcomed most of our customers, and it looked great. And when Minas finished his coffee and a nap and strode off to attend to some work around the back of the taverna, I noticed he was looking toned from all the work he'd been doing in the hot sun, his jeans hanging off him and his back nut-brown. I smiled to myself as I changed into a bikini and walked with Lisa down to the beach.

It felt as though we were getting things together. We now had enough cash to pay off the outstanding invoice for stocking the kitchen at the start of the season and, with my expenses covered, I was able to lend the business a little money to help with some other costs. Since coming back to Karpathos, I'd learned that Minas had loans to pay off as well as bills. But he was confident that when things got busy we'd be bringing in plenty of money every day, which did match what I'd seen happen at the *kantina* on Tilos. And although we were currently experiencing midsummer heat, the main influx of visitors to the island wouldn't happen until July.

Stamatis the fisherman hadn't been back yet as it was still too early in the season to make it worthwhile, given what he would have to spend on fuel to travel up from the south. So we hadn't yet been able to offer fresh fish to customers. But one evening a red and white fishing boat pulled up to the beach and two fishermen from Diafani, the port here in the north, came ashore. The older man had curly grey hair and a gold cross on a chain around his neck; his dark-haired, taciturn, twenty-year-old son wore a silver earring.

The fishermen brought octopus that they'd already tenderised, and Minas wrapped it in foil with bay leaves and olive oil and vinegar and put it on the grill over the hot coals. Then they ordered drinks, salad and potatoes and bread, and, while I went inside to work on those, Minas discussed with them what fish they were catching and agreed to buy several kilos. I was a little surprised that he agreed to spend so much while there were still few customers and while he was worried about money – but it was a necessary risk involved in running a fish taverna in the middle of nowhere, and he knew his business. He showed me what he'd bought: *skaros*, or parrotfish, some grey and some a muted red; and *melanouri*, or bream, with bright, silvery scales and marble-white meat.

When Minas judged the octopus was done, he opened the foil package, releasing a deeply aromatic steam. The men invited us to sit down with them to share it, and the meat was tender and sweet. Scooter appeared, wearing his trademark thick vest, seemingly oblivious to the fact that it was the middle of June in the South Aegean.

'We need more raki,' he said as he poured himself a large one, finishing off the bottle.

Somehow, whenever we were at our most prepared, fully stocked with fresh fish and other food, everything clean and all of us ready to work, no-one came. Whether people would drive down to the beach was purely a matter of chance; few would expect to find a taverna in such a remote place, so they wouldn't come looking for lunch. The people who did come were usually looking for an unspoiled beach, a detour off the beaten track, the kind of place you hope still exists in the world but so rarely does. The tricky, winding track, easiest to handle with a jeep or 4X4 and quite a shock when you first drive it, was the main reason the beach remained quiet and wild, and the main reason it attracted interesting people.

'The road is a filter,' said Minas. We just had to ensure people knew we were here, and that we offered them a great experience. At least on a hot day they might be pleasantly surprised to find cold drinks.

One couple arrived late in the day and decided to stay for dinner. They loved the beach and the taverna's hand-painted menu and the laid-back atmosphere. We sat with them as the sun went down behind the hills. The dusky light over the sea was calm and peaceful.

'This is such a beautiful place,' they said. 'Is there somewhere to stay?'

We had no accommodation, we explained. But Minas suggested they borrow a couple of sleeping bags and pillows from us and stay in our 'million-star hotel' on the beach, and we'd make them breakfast in the morning. Up for an adventure, they loved the idea and had a magical night. And then they booked a few nights in our hotel in the village.

HOOKED

The sun rose from behind the church on the cliff, warming the tent and gently waking me to a calm morning. I heard the wooden kitchen door being unlocked and opened, and the noise of the fridges as Minas went inside to make himself a coffee. A bit of business motivated him. I took Lisa for a pre-breakfast walk off the lead, training her to stay with me when bribed with a treat. Minas sometimes walked her too, training and teaching her things. She adored him.

After making the bread dough and leaving it to rise, I strolled down to the sea for a swim and a little time on the empty beach. Now that Scooter was responsible for the cleaning, I didn't have to do so much of the menial work. Meanwhile, every morning Minas had to explain to Scooter what he needed to do: clean the bathroom, wipe the tables, sweep the terrace, clean and mop the kitchen, put out cushions on the benches. If he trained him properly now, he told me, it would stand us in good stead when the busy days of July and August hit.

The kitchen stank to high heaven, which Minas thought was the fault of one of the machines. I hoped he would fix it after they'd finished repairing the final bench, plus one of the struts of the pergola that was leaning slightly. Minas loved the challenge of fixing things and the back of the taverna was a hospital for broken machines he intended to repair one day. The things that couldn't be revived would be plundered for parts. Not much got thrown away. He also continued to add to the décor around the place: a painting of his own, a hand-painted menu, and a picture made from driftwood by an artist from Athens, one of a group of people who often camped at the beach during the summer and had become friends with Minas over the years.

Much as I enjoyed being out of email range for a while, I was getting a little behind. I still had to deal with anything that required connectivity – bookings on Airbnb (for which the system requires timely responses), emails for my own business, bills both here and in Tilos – during my limited time up in the village, because a logistical conundrum was thwarting our attempts to instal internet at the beach. The technician needed to call us at the taverna to let us know when he was on his way to instal the satellite dish. We kept explaining that if we had a phone line or even mobile reception at the taverna, if we weren't in a remote location, we wouldn't need a satellite dish for internet; and that because we were a business, we couldn't just sit around elsewhere on the off-chance that he might call – but the message, so to speak, wasn't being received by the person sitting in a head office somewhere. Eventually the company grasped the problem and the technician showed up at the taverna one day, late in the afternoon and somewhat flustered, having not comprehended quite how far we were from town. He made a start on the installation but had to leave before the job was finished and drive all the way back down to the south of the island to catch a plane to Rhodes. He promised to return the following week.

Typically, after the fishermen's visit, none of our customers was interested in eating fish. The catch Minas had bought remained on ice in the fridge until, as I'd hoped, he offered to cook some for our dinner. It was one of the perks of living at a fish taverna. He lit the charcoal while I went for an early evening swim. Scooter had already eaten a mound of garlicky tzatziki and spent the early evening regaling us with stories of allergies he got from working in fields, and how he cured them by rubbing vinegar and white spirit on his skin. We nodded and murmured, trying to focus on other things, until at last he went to lie on his camp bed in the corner, continuing to talk to himself as he fell asleep. Minas played some game about saving the world on his tablet, depressed that he was broke. Having made a salad, I finished editing a story as the fish cooked. It was very quiet, the wind blowing the occasional bug from the fields into our drinks, Lisa curled up on her blanket and the moon shining bright above the sea, turning it silver.

In the morning, Minas took Scooter off to do some work with him and I had the taverna to myself. I enjoyed the solitude as I did the cleaning in the hot sun with Pink Floyd playing on the music system. As midday approached, a few vehicles descended the track. A tall man in Speedos walked up through the olive trees looking red and sweaty, asked for a beer and relaxed visibly as he drained an ice-cold bottle. Thankfully, Minas was back in time to cook lunch for a Greek family and an Austrian couple, as well as an Italian group he'd met on the road and encouraged to come down.

As someone who loved food, it was a pleasure to decant olive oil made from Minas's own trees; to breathe in the delicious steam as he unwrapped a fish he'd grilled with rosemary and lemon; to hear people enthuse about our bread and ask for more. We were busy for a few hours and together handled everything smoothly. I took orders, brought out drinks and mezes, and even needed to make more bread. The Italians were good fun and taught me to say *salute* when we gave them shots of raki after the meal. Since Scooter would clean up, I could relax and chat with customers. The Greeks finished the last of the fish and drank a lot of beer. It was evening when everyone left, and I went for a late swim under a beautiful, almost full moon after a satisfying day. I saw how I could get hooked on this kind of life.

❖ ❖ ❖ ❖

We'd just enjoyed a peaceful dinner, having been on the go all day, and were looking forward to an early night when Lisa barked to announce the arrival of a car. We turned to see the lights of a truck bumping down the road. It had to be Vasilis from the top of the valley. Lisa continued to inform us that someone was coming until he parked his truck and strolled in, wearing a peaked cap and carrying a five-kilo jar of goats' cheese and two kilo-jars of honey.

I brought Vasilis a beer, and he encouraged us to sit with him and chat for a while, which was indeed the welcoming thing for us to do. He insisted on buying a round of drinks, and we talked about business and had a look at the products he'd brought. The white cheese was hard, creamy and strong-tasting, the pieces nicely misshapen, while the heather honey looked and tasted like caramel. We were sure our customers would appreciate both, and for me it was wonderful. You couldn't really get more local than this.

Minas rolled himself a cigarette, scattering bits of tobacco all over the table, then lay down on the bench and soon fell asleep, leaving me and Scooter to entertain our guest. When Vasilis ordered another round I declined, saying we had to be up early; he countered that he had to be up much earlier, so I went in and grabbed a few more beers. Eventually, I took the plates and the remains of Minas's tobacco inside, topped up the olive oil bottles for the next day, and put the takings somewhere safe for the night. The boys would clean up the kitchen in the morning. When Vasilis left, Scooter and I tried to wake Minas so he could sleep somewhere more comfortable, but failed to rouse him. We covered him with a sleeping bag.

As the afternoons and evenings got busier, I didn't always get around to eating, except for the occasional surplus chip that didn't, ahem, fit on the plate. Minas was the same, which was probably why he would invariably fall asleep after dinner and a beer or two. I preferred to wait until all the work was done and the kitchen was empty, then make myself a salad of tomatoes, cucumber, onion, olives and green pepper, heaped with Vasilis's flavourful goats' cheese and sprinkled with coarse salt and oregano, drenching it with Minas's olive oil that would mingle deliciously with the juice of the tomatoes to be mopped up with bread. I'd eat while watching the moon come up red from the sea and rise over the olive trees.

Finally, the technician returned to finish installing our satellite dish, which would give us not only internet but also a phone line of sorts once Minas figured out how to set it up. This made my visits to the village somewhat less stressful – getting online was one thing I no longer had to worry about. All I had to do on my next drive up was see the carpenter about ordering new signs, walk down to the valley and dig up some mint to plant at the beach, pick up some tobacco for Minas, clean the rooms of course, meet the new guests, wash and press laundry… As a break, I went for iced coffee at Archontoula's. Having errands to run and work to do made me feel part of the community. It always took a while to leave, and I was usually loaded down with an assortment of things that needed ferrying back and forth.

'How are you getting to the beach?' asked Yiannis the cobbler.

'How's business?' asked Rigopoula, standing at her shop. 'Is the water running down at Ayios Minas? Is your dog keeping the goats away from my olive trees?'

'Come and sit down and have a cold drink,' said Sophia, inviting me into her café at the entrance to the village.

I sat for a while at Sophia's, eating yoghurt and honey and walnuts, waiting for a tour bus to arrive. Minas had asked the driver, a friend of his, to bring a five-kilo bag of lamb chops from the butcher in town to save him a trip. Driving to town was another cost to be factored in to our budget, given the price of fuel. I met the bus, secured the bag of meat carefully, packed it into the Lada with everything else and drove down to the beach.

There was only one table of customers, so later that evening we made the most of the situation by cooking up all the fish we had left over that day: *barbounia*, red mullet, with their crisp rosy skin and sweet white flesh, grilled with slices of lemon and sprigs of rosemary; *sargos*, sea bream; grey and red *skaros*, sweetened with tomato and onion. It was a treat, but Minas was frustrated by the lack of business. He got stressed when there was no-one to cook for – when people left the beach without coming to the taverna.

'I don't know how you can stay so calm,' he said, 'when you don't even smoke, or drink much.' But I could escape from time to time, go for a swim or take Lisa for a walk up the valley. And of course, it didn't mean the same to me; he'd poured his heart and soul and income into the taverna for years.

He was getting impatient with Scooter. It sometimes seemed we were paying him to do nothing except talk about how much better things were elsewhere, both in Albania and in Diafani where he used to work. I did lose my cool too, sometimes, when I saw Scooter sitting around doing nothing to earn his keep and getting in my way or telling me what to do.

Part of this was a misunderstanding on my part. There's a Greek expression, '*Kaneh tin douleia sou*', which means literally 'Do your work'. What I only realised much later is that the true meaning of the phrase is more like, 'Take your time, feel free to finish what you're doing.' But when I thought Scooter was telling me to do my work, I was fuming. 'It's not my work!' I retorted, probably baffling him.

(I also learned around that time that when people asked, '*Echei douleia?*' – literally meaning 'Is there work?' – they meant 'Do you have any business?' I was confused at first: of course there was work, there was always work…)

The next morning, I heard Minas cursing Scooter.

'What happened?' I asked.

'I asked him if he knew how to paint a wall yesterday and he said he did. I gave him the paint, and the thinner for cleaning the brush after. I needed the thinner this morning so I asked him where it was. He said he'd mixed it all in with the paint, half and half…'

He sighed. Replenishing supplies of a simple thing like paint thinner would take an hour each way driving to town. And the paint on the wall was so thin it was almost transparent.

Scooter, believing he'd been unfairly reprimanded, sat in the taverna and sulked. Meanwhile, he still hadn't planted the seeds for the little vegetable garden we wanted to make. I'd brought some seed packets I had at home in Tilos and planned to plant them myself once we were organised, but Minas said Scooter was good at it and I agreed we should give him jobs to do that he liked. I felt a little sorry for him when he looked bored. Yet he still hadn't done anything with them. Moreover, he still hadn't planted the mint I'd walked all the way down to the riverbed to find after cleaning rooms in the village. When I expressed my discontent, Minas planted the mint himself in next to no time and got Scooter to start digging the ground for seeds. It kept them occupied for a while.

In the afternoon, I was in the kitchen preparing the cutlery and breadbasket for a couple who had ordered beers and salads when

Scooter pointlessly gestured towards the fresh bread I'd made, saying, 'Give them this bread, it's better' – as if it hadn't occurred to me and I needed his instructions. I flew at him. Minas, in an effort to keep the peace, suggested I take a cold beer to the beach, and I did. He could handle things himself.

After the customers had left, feeling a little bad for losing my temper with Scooter and thinking we all might need a break, I suggested we drive to Diafani for the evening. Minas needed to buy tobacco again anyway – he was always running out, half of it spilling and blowing all over the tables – and it would be useful to drop off the rubbish. Most importantly, he and Scooter could go and see their various friends.

Minas agreed it was a nice idea, and turned on the hot water heater so he could take a shower. When he re-emerged, the dark stubble was gone, as was the now standard daytime outfit of baseball cap, oversized football T-shirt and, not particularly flattering but certainly practical, long baggy shorts and kitchen clogs. Dressed for an outing, he was in a classic Greek blue striped shirt, jeans that trailed slightly around his black leather shoes – and, of course, a roll-up cigarette in his mouth, made with the last of his tobacco. He fixed a coffee to take for the drive – the Lada was full of old coffee cups – and insisted we stop at the church on the way to light a candle. 'Maybe that's why there's no business, we haven't lit candles for the miracle worker,' he said. 'Let's light a whole barbecue...'

Unfortunately, Scooter had to sit in the back of the Lada with the smelly rubbish bags that had been waiting, full of fish bones, for a couple of days. Plus, Minas had been having a bit of a clear-out during the quiet days, and the seat-less back of the car was stuffed with junk, so Scooter was wedged into a little corner at a weird angle, sitting on a crate, banging his head on the roof whenever we went over a bump. But he didn't seem to mind.

It took over half an hour to drive from Ayios Minas to the port, even with Minas behind the wheel: a few kilometres up to the road, along the ridge towards Olympos and then turning off down a winding road again to the sea. Diafani was a fishing village built along a mostly pebble beach, with its ferry dock (now repaired) extending into the sea; behind the cluster of houses, green slopes rose to high limestone peaks. While it lacked the beauty of Olympos, it boasted half a dozen tavernas overlooking the sea, some simple hotels, and walking paths in various directions; the only shop at the time was a very tired-looking place run by an old couple who sat on chairs out in the alley. We parked and told Scooter we'd see him later.

An old lady called Anna ran the traditional kafeneio, and had the distinction of being the only person to sell cigarettes and tobacco in the months when the seafront kiosk was closed. Taking her responsibility seriously, she was very cautious about letting anyone take more than their fair share, and kept them in a wooden cabinet in the little café along with the chocolate. We went in and had coffee, running into someone who calculated he was a second cousin of Minas, and then we went for a drink at another bar to see other friends of his. It was good PR, Minas said, to remind locals we were open.

We'd only been sitting down for ten minutes when Scooter showed up and joined us. He couldn't be bothered to talk to all the friends he'd been bragging about if they weren't offering him work. Thankfully, all the bars and restaurants in the port were quiet, so at least it made Minas feel better about our lack of business.

❖ ❖ ❖ ❖

Lisa rolled around on the pebbles, scratching her back. The water was a rippling topaz blue. I threw a stick into the sea and she swam in to fetch it a few times, then when she'd cooled off I left her sitting by the water's edge chewing the stick while I swam. She'd look over to check how I was doing in the water, and when I got out she wagged her tail. If I lay down, she came to sit by me so I would rub her chest. Even when I read a book, I still had one hand free, after all.

Ever since she was two months old, Lisa and I had walked together from my village house to beaches where she would cool off from the summer heat in the sea. When I got dressed to leave and said, 'Let's go!' she would cast a look over at the water, clearly communicating that she wanted to stay. If I didn't relent, she avoided my eyes and slowly sat down again. Sometimes I gave in and we stayed a bit longer. But if I insisted we were going home, she'd bound up the beach, pulling me along on the end of the lead.

By late June, though, there wasn't time to linger at the beach. The bookings for rooms were coming in thick and fast, and I resolved to put together a proper calendar for the coming busy months so we could plan the week. More bookings meant more driving up to the village and more cleaning; summer brought dust, too, which I had to wash from the exterior woodwork, the doors and shutters and balustrades. But I enjoyed days when I didn't have to rush back. I could now call to check everything was under control, because Minas had finally managed to hook up the phone at the taverna. In fact, most of the first calls were from his mother – he was a Greek man, after all. '*Ela Mama*, hi Mom… Yeah, I'm a bit busy right now, can I call you back?'

On a day when he said he'd had some business but nothing he couldn't handle with Scooter, I decided to stay in the village for the night again. It was time to venture into the kitchen of his house – he'd given me the key to the final frontier, the final awful secret. If I didn't mind cleaning it up, I could use it whenever I liked, which would allow me to work in peace rather than in a busy café surrounded by distractions. I stepped inside and shuddered. Among mouldy coffee mugs, broken glass, dirty clothes, clumps of tobacco, bags of rubbish, rotten onions in the cupboard and unidentifiable objects in the fridge, I also found lovely, creative signs he had hand-painted for the hotel. It was a delightful kitchen, with a window looking out over the sea, and it felt good to make it habitable again. Now there were no more locked doors.

At 5pm, I waited at Sophia's café for the latest guests to arrive, some Czech windsurfers who were driving up from the south. Sophia made a good Greek coffee and gave me lovely *biskotakia* to go with it. The TV was on in the background, the parrot was whistling, and a group of locals were chatting about business while Sophia cooked or did her embroidery, sitting by the door. I was still waiting for the guests an hour later, so Sophia fed me fava and some heavenly fried courgettes – thinly sliced, very sweet, with a tiny sprinkling of salt. She asked if Minas was paying me properly, and I told her we had an arrangement that worked for me.

Originally, I was happy to help out in return for a place to live with all my (and Lisa's) expenses paid. As the weeks had passed, however, and I'd become more involved in the day-to-day running of both hotel and taverna, we'd discussed the arrangement again. If I decided to leave at the end of the summer and go back home to Tilos, Minas would pay me whatever we agreed was fair – a kind of end-of-season bonus – but if I decided to stay longer, we could live between the taverna and the hotel, and the business would go some way to supporting us for the winter. I liked my editorial work – but not working as much, having time to write and to go walking, was even better. In the meantime, I was enjoying spending less time sitting at a desk in front of a computer screen. And although Minas was sometimes impossible, he was often wonderful.

The windsurfers arrived and I took them to their room, then walked to the end of the village. I looked up at the line of stone windmills on the mist-covered ridge, with beautiful flashes of sunlight through the clouds covering the mountaintops; down the slope was a white chapel, its steps snaking down the cliff, and the sea far below. It was oddly nice, when it was midsummer-hot down at the beach, to come up to a breezy, cool day on the mountain, and wear my comfy walking boots as a change from sandals. I'd catch up on laundry and enjoy a quiet workspace.

'*Eh*, *kaleh*!' shouted Maroukla the next morning with a forthright greeting, as if surprised to see me. 'Your light was on late last night. When did you arrive?'

I explained that I was up late working at my computer. As if she didn't already know – she saw everything. Often as soon as I stepped out of the door I'd hear a shout and see her waving to me from her yard.

I waited until the guests checked out so I could get the rooms ready again. While doing a last lot of washing, I cleaned the yard of Minas's house. Its beautiful purple bougainvillaea shed heaps of petals that gathered in the corners along with anything else the wind brought in. I swept up, wiped the table and bench, and cleared out the border with the plants. It would be better hanging up the laundry in a clean courtyard.

'Bravo!' said Georgia next door, as her customers now had a more attractive view from her café's panoramic terrace. Georgia was another of Minas's cousins, the slightly younger sister of Evgenia, with long dark hair and long eyelashes. I waved to her as I left the village in the middle of the afternoon.

Minas had dropped me off the day before so he could have use of the Lada. I set off walking and was offered a ride by a couple of young guys who had been doing work on the electrical lines in the village. The driver, who enjoyed the opportunity to speak English, told me he loved his job as he got to travel all over the islands. When we reached the turn off, he insisted on driving me all the way to the beach. As we made our way down the narrow track, he told me they'd had fun working in the village all day as they'd been offered glass after glass of raki and beer. I laughed nervously and tried not to think about that as I looked at the sheer drops at either side, then was careful not to distract him. We made it in one piece, and the guys came in for another beer.

Leaving my bag on the bench by the kitchen, I said hi to Minas, who was dressed in a bright red T-shirt several sizes too big, stained with grease and soot from the barbecue. I asked if he needed any help.

'No, I'm fine… now.'

'What d'you mean?'

'Go for a swim, I'll tell you later.'

I learned that I'd missed a drama that afternoon.

The canvas covering over the pergola flapped in the breeze at the best of times, acting like a sail. Today had been exceptionally windy, and a huge gust had been seriously threatening to pull the pergola away.

Minas had scrambled up on to the wall by the barbecue and grabbed the beam above tightly to pull himself up on to the roof. Suddenly he'd felt a searing pain. He'd leapt back down to find a fish hook in the flesh of his palm by the thumb. It took three men to remove it and he'd almost fainted. He'd cursed Scooter, who always left things in odd places and must have stuck the hook in the wood.

'Oh my goodness… Are you OK?'

'Yeah, I had a shot of raki and it'll be fine. It was bad, though… And where did he find a massive fish hook?!'

I hesitated.

'You know last week,' I said, 'when the fishermen brought up that huge grouper they caught using octopus as bait? Well, when I was cleaning up later, I found a big fish hook and wasn't sure what to do with it, and I thought it would make a good decoration given that we're a fish taverna. So I, er, stuck it into the wood over the barbecue…'

It's one way to hook a man.

Thankfully he laughed.

BIRTHDAY

The wind blew powerfully down the valley, knocking chairs over on the taverna terrace. I'd put rocks in the corners of my tent to hold it down. The old bamboo roof creaked and the thick canvas flapped like a sail. Minas as always left his tobacco pouch lying on a table, in complete denial about the wind and the fact that we lived so far from anywhere selling tobacco, but even he put something heavy on the pouch to stop it blowing away. I could see now why we needed wood to complete the pergola, and more glass windows to close off the back of the restaurant. But all that cost money and, although it was early July, there was still precious little coming in. Meanwhile, there was something beautiful about the yellow-painted taverna with its low stone-and-wood walls being open to the olive trees all around, the shrub-covered hills.

Minas's mood was better now that a few cars were coming to the beach every day, and people of various nationalities would stop in, either walking up through the field from the beach or parking their car behind the taverna. 'Smile and Wave' was his mantra when potential customers approached.

'Welcome!' he'd say if they came in, and not put them under any pressure. If they sat down, he'd ask 'So are you hungry, or thirsty, or both?'

Four French holidaymakers came in one day and ordered one beer and a plate of fried potatoes between them; but the man in the green shirt remembered having a mojito here four years earlier, so Minas made them a carafe of raki mojito on the house using our newly planted spearmint and Vasilis's honey. It was these touches of hospitality that made people want to return.

Almost every day, as we smiled and waved, we'd see someone approach looking troubled. On one typical occasion, an Italian man entered the taverna and said, 'I have one question.'

'Yes?' I asked, though I already knew what it was.

'Which road is better?'

There were two dirt tracks down to the valley. One was a kilometre shorter than the other, but steeper and not ideal for an ordinary car; I'd never attempted that one in the Lada, though it was the one Minas used when he drove to town. The other, past the church, was slightly less hair-raising and met the road closer to the village, so I always took that one. Both were winding and narrow with switchbacks and sheer drops. Either could be a shock first time around, especially if you weren't used to driving in mountainous terrain. The Swiss didn't mind it too much, but the Dutch could be reduced to tears.

'What kind of car are you driving?' I asked. 'Is it a jeep or a Fiat Panda?'

'No, no...' He indicated it was some other kind of small rental car.

'Which road did you come down?' I continued, though sadly I knew the likely answer.

'This,' he said, pointing to the church.

I had to break it to him that the one he'd been shaken by – and hoped to avoid on the way back – was the better of the two roads.

In fact, people drove so carefully there was never an accident, unlike on busy roads in every city in Europe. You just had to take it slowly and look ahead for cars coming the other way. But one of the first Italian phrases I picked up that summer was *la strada è pericolosa*: the road is dangerous. I once made the mistake of joking, 'It's not dangerous; though if you drove off it, that would be dangerous.' It was the wrong thing to say. People just wanted to be reassured.

'We have a solution,' piped up Minas.

'Yes?' said the man with a glimmer of hope in his eye, nervous but wanting to believe, ready to give up his first-born rather than brave not just the road but his wife's displeasure.

'Yes!' said Minas. 'Your wife is scared, yes?'

I knew from personal experience that it was easier to drive the road than be a helpless passenger.

'Yes….' replied the man, shaking his head as he remembered the dressing down he'd received and how this really wasn't how he wanted to spend his holiday.

'Bring her and we will give you the solution for the road,' said Minas, calmly.

The man was sceptical but willing to try anything. He went to bring his still flustered wife from the car. Minas gave me the nod. I went inside feeling slightly guilty and came back out with an unmarked bottle from the freezer and two shot glasses.

'No, no!' said the woman who'd appeared through the doorway. 'He can't, he is driving.'

'Relax, darling,' said Minas. 'Just one finger, I promise. It will help.' They still looked unconvinced. I filled the glasses as Minas added, 'It's my birthday.'

'Birthday…?' asked the couple, brightening. 'Ah, happy birthday!' Suddenly smiling, they felt this was a lucky day to have come here. It was a happy place.

Sipping at the raki they relaxed, laughing. They would leave with fond memories. Maybe the drive back wouldn't be so bad after all. This man had celebrated many birthdays here. They had no idea… He celebrated his birthday every day. Raki was one of the most important tools of the trade.

The first Greek campers arrived, having heard about the place on the free-camping circuit. Free camping was unofficially tolerated on certain beaches on certain islands, and was a good way for people to escape the furnace heat of cities in the summer and live close to the sea for a month or two. This quiet, youngish couple bought a meal per day and water and in return could use our bathroom and shower and internet. They spent the first evening on the windy terrace glued to their tablets.

Thanks to the wind, it was cool enough outside that I could wear jeans and walking boots, but it was impossible to stay long in the heat of the kitchen dressed like that. There was only one small screened vent high up on the wall, and the fridges and freezer radiated more heat than the oven and gas rings and griddle. On the campers' second night, I read a book on the terrace while Minas contentedly prepared us an excellent, juicy pastitsio, pasta baked with tomato and meat sauce, along with a salad of cucumber, rocket, onion, green pepper, goats' cheese and olives. Afterwards, he tried to watch a football game online on my laptop with the campers but the slow internet made it hard to be engrossed. The couple said goodnight early and went to bed.

Business was slow for a few days, cash flow tight. We'd need to pay Scooter his first month's wages soon. Things were looking precarious again and I worried slightly about getting my little loan repaid if things continued this way, though my few hundred euros was nothing compared to what Minas had invested in his taverna over the years. I reminded him that he'd been away the previous summer and people might not know we were open. It didn't matter nearly so much to me, but in an informal way I was happy to help him manage things and on a personal level I couldn't help wanting to make a success of it. We were a team. There was nothing official – I certainly wasn't an equal partner, it was Minas's business – but it certainly felt as though we were working towards a common goal.

'We made a grand total of what, ten bucks this lunchtime?' said Minas. 'Thank god for the campers… What are their names?'

'I can't remember,' I said sheepishly, though they'd been staying at the beach for a few days now. He laughed. Even when we had a really good time with visitors and enjoyed getting to know them, it was hard to remember names when everyone came and went in a few days. I saw the names Ursula and Jurgen in my notebook and tried in vain to recall what they looked like. I did remember a couple of Italians who'd arrived by motorbike in June, a big bear of a man and a petite woman who smoked cigars. Minas had offered to make pizza and they'd argued in a good-humoured way about how to make it, and I'd taken photos. I decided to start a Facebook page for the taverna and maybe put guest photos on it.

Thankfully, given the taverna was quiet, we had a regular flow of guests staying in the hotel. I told Minas I was happy to keep cleaning the rooms to save money on hiring someone. It wouldn't make sense to take on someone full-time and there didn't seem to be anyone available for the few hours we needed them, typically the middle of the day between check-out and check-in, which coincided with the hours when restaurants and shops were busiest. The cleaning could only be done later or earlier in the day if there was a gap between bookings.

I left one morning while the sea was a silver shimmer and the hills deep green; drove up the winding, bumpy dirt track in the rusty Lada, then along the mountain ridge to the village. It must have been one of the most beautiful commutes in the world and I'd got used to driving up the crazy road.

'You see this view every day?' asked an Italian couple meandering down the alleyway who paused at the gate of Minas's house, as so many people did, and took photos of the bougainvillaea-covered balcony with the sea far below and rugged cliffs tailing off into the distance.

'Yes,' I replied, smiling. It was still a pleasure, though at that moment I was struggling with a load of sheets and towels that needed washing, drying and pressing. I had to rush to talk to the carpenter about supplying wood to finish off the roof and windows, see Minas's uncle Antonis about some vegetables, and collect money from his uncle Nick.

All this was good practice for my Greek, as was the fact that Minas and I spoke in Greek some of the time; although, as with any learning, I made my fair share of mistakes. When Minas mentioned a *prosfora* I thought he wanted me to ask the carpenter for a discount – I'd only ever seen the word in shop windows advertising sales – and, a little embarrassed to be so bold, asked the carpenter instead for 'a good price'. I didn't realise that in this context, *prosfora* meant quotation. Still, maybe the carpenter thought I was a tough businesswoman, like all the women in the village…

Back down at the beach, while dinner cooked over the charcoal, I had a glass of wine or two in the breeze and quiet, sitting at my computer setting up the taverna Facebook page while Minas painted a picture of the bay on a new sign to put up on the beach. Moments like this felt good – cut off from the world. This place was beginning to feel like home; I had settled in, and Minas and I got along very well, appreciating one another's different forms of creativity. Lisa seemed contented too, especially now she had two men feeding her treats and taking her for walks. At eight thirty in the evening, a bright white almost-full moon shone high above in a pink and pale-blue sky. A wild wind was blowing through the olive trees and the pines. Just as we were ready to turn in, Vasilis arrived with a delivery of cheese and honey, and a thirst. I had a few drinks with him – after all, we needed the business.

Even though I knew Vasilis well by now, I still sometimes found it difficult to understand what he was saying. The next morning, I mentioned this to Minas and he said not to worry, he didn't always understand him either. It was best just to answer, '*Echeis dikio*' – you're right. He also said in this community everyone was always giving advice and telling you to do things this way or that, or telling you their crazy beliefs. Instead of getting exasperated or arguing, the best response was: 'I never thought of it that way before.' It was actually a great coping mechanism.

After a quick morning swim, I got on with my own work for a few hours since I didn't have to drive up to the village and Minas could take care of the taverna. I had a breakfast of fresh bread with the cream cheese Minas had made using milk and a little yoghurt, which tasted delicious with a touch of Vasilis's heather honey. Minas was explaining to Scooter the morning routine for the umpteenth time when there was a mini-panic as we discovered everything in the main food fridge was warm. Something must have broken. And during the night the ferocious wind had torn apart the cables for the lights over half the restaurant. It would keep the boys busy for the morning, mending everything.

Funnily enough, on a day when there so was so much to fix that we didn't feel properly prepared, lunchtime was a success, with customers of various nationalities enthusing over lamb chops and salads, taking photos of the fish on the grill and the stuffed calamari. When people liked it here, they loved it: the place was paradise and everything tasted delicious, and the positive energy was infectious. Minas showed people my books and someone bought one. He celebrated his birthday and got tipsy, but in late afternoon things calmed down – and I found flowers stashed in my laptop.

❖ ❖ ❖ ❖

Just as it looked as if business was picking up, the next morning some guys arrived with a white shipping container and dumped it in the field next to the beach. Minas told me the neighbours had arrived.

Since we'd had the valley to ourselves until now, it came as a surprise, although he must have mentioned it: just two minutes' walk back from ours was another taverna. It didn't actually look like a taverna, but that's because it was still closed, with everything packed away: it only opened in the busiest months of summer, which were now around the corner. Unfortunately, perhaps because this taverna had been established before Minas's and the owners saw him as unwanted competition rather than adding to the appeal of the beach, apparently they didn't much like Minas being here. He might have been hoping they wouldn't open this year, as the couple had other jobs for the rest of the year, but it now looked as though they would.

The neighbours came and left for now, but the white container lay like a badly parked spaceship, mysterious and incongruous, in the corner of the field where the riverbed met the beach and where many visitors left their vehicles. Minas made a call to the owner of the field, and a few others; it seemed that the owners of the other taverna were going to use it as a *kantina* or kiosk for serving drinks on the beach. This would be disastrous for Minas, as fewer people would come and find us. Minas didn't want all of the business – he just wanted some of it.

Although neither the spaceship nor the other taverna had opened yet, it seemed there might be trouble ahead, judging from Minas's mood. By late morning, he'd already cracked open his first beer. He should have been in his element over an unusually busy lunchtime with some Swiss people who arrived on one of the small excursion boats from Diafani, and return customers from Austria, all of them hungry; but he remained subdued and untalkative. When the Swiss wanted to pay their bill online, the online credit card system wouldn't work, which didn't help matters. He was not in a cheerful frame of mind when his cousin Evgenia called to say she was on her way back from town, had picked up some supplies for us and, although she couldn't drive down as she was in a big rush, would stop and wait if we drove up to meet her at the road in ten to fifteen minutes.

I offered to do it as he was busy cooking and it would be a relief to get away from the gloomy atmosphere.

I drove up fast, making it in twelve minutes from the church, feeling pleased to be efficient and helpful. There was no sign of Evgenia yet but I was happy to have a rest. The wind was blowing and rustling the pine trees on the other side of the ridge. I waited for a while, then thought it was odd she hadn't arrived. Eventually I wondered if she was waiting at the top of the other track – but Minas knew I never drove up the other, steeper track as I didn't feel confident handling it. Surely he would have told her which track to wait at? Finally she called, and she was indeed at the top of the other track. I found her, we transferred stuff from her truck to the Lada very fast, and I drove back down.

'Why were you at the wrong road?' asked Minas testily.

Flustered and upset, since I'd only been trying to help and it wasn't my fault, I got on with serving customers, trying to ignore the tension, which wasn't easy – though smiling and laughing and chatting with people helped. I forgot to charge one table for the bread when I made up their bill; then Minas forgot to check if the octopus was cooked through before he served it. But all the customers enjoyed themselves and the shots of raki we gave them afterwards – for Minas's birthday, of course. He encouraged me to have a Fix, our house beer, and as usual it fixed things. The anger both of us felt had passed.

The fishermen arrived to spend the night in the bay, and talked with Minas about the odd white container in the field. The campers came for a beer, mainly so they could charge their phones and use the toilet and shower. I cleaned up a little while Minas watered the seedlings we had planted. With the wind blowing there were few mosquitoes, and the cool air was good for sleeping. Crawling into the tent was as delicious as expected.

I woke to blue skies, feeling happy and rested even though a fierce wind was still flapping the tent around. Lisa looked over expectantly, wagging her tail, from the tree where she was tethered by a long lead. Scooter was actually washing the kitchen floor, which was quite astonishing. There was no system to what he did: sometimes instead of checking if everything was clean and in place in the morning, he just wandered off to the beach or fed Lisa, while we went round trying to put things in their proper place after he'd left them here or there. When he couldn't remember where to put something, he didn't ask – he just left it in a sink.

For the first time in ages, I cooked myself one of my favourite breakfasts, frying up courgette, pepper and onion, and eggs with runny yolks. We had a whole restaurant kitchen at our disposal and Minas was more than happy for any of us to cook whatever we liked for ourselves. I felt a little guilty leaving the washing up for Scooter, then reminded myself that was what we paid him for. Thinking I'd take photos for our Facebook page, I went for a walk on to the headland to the right, where a path to a small cove offered glorious views of the whole beach and the aquamarine waters below. A very bronzed couple were sunbathing by the cliffs.

By lunchtime there was no sign of business – it was certainly quiet for July, though it was still early in the month – but Minas finished painting a beautiful sign for the hotel while I uploaded photos to the Facebook page and tested the new pancake recipe with banana and a drizzle of local honey. I took Lisa for another walk while Minas used my laptop to design a poster and Scooter slept in a chair. We were waiting for a delivery of wood to finish off the roof and the walls, which at least would be something to occupy the boys – though we didn't have the money yet for glass windows. As the day wore on, more cars drove down to the beach but the only visitor was a local guy demanding money Minas apparently owed him for work he had done.

Eventually, a table of Dutch people arrived wanting to eat, and while they waited Minas suggested they paint stones, a tradition he started years ago. People would bring a flat pebble or rock from the beach and use our paints to create their own piece of art, usually signing and dating it to leave on the walls around the terrace as a kind of guest book. When I'd first arrived and he asked me to pick up the fallen stones and arrange them on the walls, I wondered what the fuss was all about, but now I saw how much people enjoyed doing the painting, something we hardly ever have time to do as grown-ups. Years later people would come and try to find the stones they'd painted.

'We don't know how to paint!' said the Dutch diners at first. But once they started, they became so absorbed in the activity that they asked us to hold off serving the meals until the stones were finished.

In the meantime, a young Italian couple came to borrow a corkscrew for a bottle of organic wine they'd brought to enjoy on the beach. We actually didn't have one, I realised, as our wine was bought in bulk, not bottles (Minas's own wine was running low, and was now reserved for special occasions).

'I'm sure we can find a solution,' I said.

While the couple looked around, noticing the tent, intrigued to find that we actually lived here, Minas and Scooter resourcefully managed to open the wine bottle using a large screw, a pair of pliers and the arm of a chair. Minas also insisted on making the couple some *patatakia* – potatoes sliced very thin using the mandolin, cooked to a crisp in the deep-fat fryer and sprinkled with a mix of salt and pepper and oregano – to take away in a paper cup, and the couple poured us each a glass of their wine.

Minas had his mojo back, the real reason people came here. He asked me to serve a round of raki to the Dutch while he gave them a rendition of 'Simple Man'. They swayed to the music, and gave him a loud cheer at the end. Scooter sat in the corner looking unimpressed.

The taverna still looked a little unfinished, with a billowing canvas for shade and a few mismatched, half-broken chairs. But it felt to me as though the summer season was beginning. And Captain Nikos was arriving from Diafani in his boat the next day, bringing with him two of Minas's best friends, Tim and Alison.

There were three excursion boats from Diafani – simple fishing boats that carried a dozen or so passengers. In July and August, or whenever they had enough customers to make it worth the cost of running, they'd take people down the coast to nearby beaches for the day, as well as all the way north to the abandoned island of Saria. Pot-bellied, steely-eyed Captain Nikos not only ran boat trips and had his own hotel, but was in charge of ferry tickets at the port and understood – as much as anyone could really understand them – the mysteries of the good ship *Prevelis*'s erratic ferry schedule. Known to Minas simply as *Kapetanios*, he was something of an institution in the north of the island and well liked by many of the regular visitors to Diafani.

Tim and Alison, an English couple from London who'd lived in Asia for years, spent six weeks of every summer in Diafani. They loved the out-of-the-way beach of Ayios Minas and had known and supported Minas since the early days when the taverna was just a hippie shack; he'd talked a lot about them and now I was finally meeting them. Tim, a retired foreign correspondent for the BBC with a laid-back charm, was very tall and thin with tousled white hair, and dressed in T-shirt and baggy Thai fisherman's pants. Alison, with boyishly short, spiky hair and an impish smile, wore grey linen and silver jewellery.

Like Minas, Tim loved his music, to play guitar and sing. So on that first visit of the summer, they spent some time on the beach and then came up for a little impromptu show. Alison lounged on the wall in the corner, reading and sipping at beer with ice and lemon. Tim sat hunched over his guitar playing old rock songs while Minas stood next to him singing, unshaven, wearing his baggy T-shirt back to front by mistake. An Italian couple having lunch were delighted by the music and got up to dance, while a family sat with drinks painting stones. A young Slovenian couple arrived by jeep and delivered a poster made by friends who had been here a couple of years ago, showing photos of them with Minas and a handwritten message about happy memories.

Tim and Alison agreed to come back the following Saturday and try to bring friends. Tim's music was well known locally, making him another crucial member of the team. Minas vowed to get the taverna in better shape by the time of the first scheduled performance.

It seemed the day couldn't get any better, but we heard a distinctive shout: '*Chronia polla!*' Stamatis was back. We turned to see him walking up the path through the field barefoot, a basket of fish on his shoulder. Just as Minas had his birthday every day, so Stamatis always greeted us with the Greek equivalent of 'Many happy returns'. He celebrated every day he woke up.

Minas was happy, sad, overwhelmed. All his friends were returning.

❖ ❖ ❖ ❖

In the heat of midday, the sun was glinting off the rocks on the beach and the sea was a vibrant blue. I had a swim then walked back to the taverna just as a group of very hot, tired people arrived. Two Italian couples and their teenage children had left their vehicles at the road, deciding to walk down the track to the beach. The sign on the road said '2km', but in fact it was at least three. They were pleased with their adventure, though, and, while they sipped on cold drinks, Minas promised to drive them back up to their vehicles when they were ready.

As they relaxed on the beach, they saw the white wooden fishing boat moor up beside them, and Stamatis jumped out carrying a grouper weighing several kilos, along with several other large fish he'd just pulled from the sea. Grouper – *rofos* in Greek, *cernia* in Italian

– are a very dark brown speckled with green or yellow, have large heads and jaws, and grow to an impressive size in these waters. The Italians took photographs, followed Stamatis up to the taverna and asked if they could reserve the two largest grouper for dinner. They were excited about making their walking adventure worthwhile, an opportunity to eat the freshest fish in this mesmerising place.

We had laughed when I was setting up the taverna Facebook page and the programme asked if we took dinner reservations; but now we did. We weighed the fish and agreed the price with one of the Italian men, who then found a large flat stone on the beach, brought it up to the shady terrace and sat for an hour or more carefully painting a picture of the fish they would eat.

That same afternoon, we had another notable arrival at the beach. Maria from Athens wore large sunglasses, red lipstick and big gold earrings, and a long scarf trailed behind her in the wind as she drew up to the back of the taverna astride an ATV with camping gear stowed neatly around her. An attractive and intelligent woman of around forty, she spent the afternoon meticulously setting up her tent. Then in the early evening she came up and ordered a glass of raki with ice, plus fish and salad to eat. I noticed her polka-dot nails.

Scooter cleaned all the fish – at last, he seemed to have got the hang of it – and Minas found some good music on the radio as he set the charcoal burning. There was a lovely light in the olive trees and on the grey flanks of the hills. We prepared salads and potatoes while the Italians had showers and drank a little cold white wine and enjoyed the cool breeze. Cooking large grouper took skill, and you couldn't mess it up – you couldn't just conjure up another one and do it again, and a large fish cost a lot of money – but Minas gave it his full attention and grilled it to perfection. The meal was a fine celebration of a memorable day for the families. At the end, we made them desserts on the house, served with shots of raki for Minas's birthday.

When the time came for him to drive everyone back up the track, it was thankfully dark so they couldn't see that the Lada was only held together with rust. Still, it must have been obvious that there were only two actual seats and the back was rather dirty with a slight odour of rubbish... Plus the driver was not completely sober. But it was all part of the experience.

Maria remained in the taverna for a while. She confessed to me that although it was wonderful to have the beach to herself, she had been hoping to meet some other campers for company. What she didn't really have in mind that night was meeting Scooter in his grey woolly vest and being regaled with the 100 Best Things About Albania. But it seems that's what she got.

When Maria quietly mentioned the next day that she hadn't really appreciated being propositioned by the cleaning staff, Minas gave him a talking to. Scooter grumpily complained the woman was mad anyway. And then, coincidentally just after he'd been paid for the month, he simply disappeared and didn't come back.

LUNCH AND LIVE MUSIC

I was happy to see the back of Scooter; apart from anything else, the last thing we needed was bored-looking staff, and he seemed more trouble than he was worth. It did leave us without any help, though. When we woke up, we were back to cleaning the tables, kitchen and bathroom ourselves, slightly more challenging now that the days were busier, with later nights and earlier mornings.

Vasilis came to deliver goats' cheese late in the evening now that there were people around to chat with. As July progressed and a few more campers arrived, Maria finally had the kind of stimulating company she'd hoped for – the kind of people who wanted to practice yoga on the beach and discuss alternative therapies – but it also meant the taverna had to be ship-shape in time to offer coffee and breakfast. For me, there were no more naps on the beach, and no long walks, since Minas could need help at any moment. We weren't working all that hard but there was little downtime – we were tied to the taverna. I began to get very tired and the only way to cope was to stay upbeat and work together well. Still, I'd rather be doing things than sitting around bored, and I liked the physical work for a change. I was certainly feeling fit.

As usual, I got up when the sun rose over the church on the cliffs. Lisa was waiting for me as always, and we ran through the field of olive trees down to the beach, jumping in the clear blue sea. Coming back, I remembered that the figs were ripe on the tree where I usually hung the laundry, and grabbed a few, warm from the sun, for breakfast. I made bread dough, measuring cups of Cretan flour from the large sacks and using our secret ingredient, sea water. I put tea bags into a bottle and left it out in the sun, for making iced tea. Then I wolfed down a bowl of yoghurt with local honey to give me energy for the day ahead.

With no-one to help us, now when I went to the village I had to be as fast as possible.

'How are you? Running again?!' asked friends I encountered along the alley.

I quickly got the day's gossip from the ladies sitting sewing outside their shops near the square, then hurried to clean the rooms, decant some olive oil from the barrels in Minas's house for the taverna, buy potatoes, meet the new hotel guests, pick up money and buy some colourful cloth in a local design from Rigopoula for our benches.

'How's the water pressure for our olive trees?' Rigopoula asked. I said I'd check.

Everyone gave me messages to take down to Minas.

'Tell him to treat you well!'

'Be careful driving down that dangerous road!'

Getting back to the beach was always a huge relief. So it wasn't much fun to get a call from Uncle Nick, saying he needed a spare key for the one of the rooms. When we weren't there, guests picked up keys and dropped them off at his taverna. I got in the Lada and drove back, quickly walked all the way through the village hoping not to have to explain to everyone why I was back – only to find he was mistaken, confused. Probably he'd had one too many rakis. I sighed, turned around, drove down again and went straight to the beach. The days were getting hot, and there were folks playing petanque wearing only a very deep suntan. Diving into the cool sea, I swam across the bay and got my equilibrium back.

We had good business through the afternoon, which Minas celebrated by drinking a lot. At the end of the day he turned the music up extremely loud, leaving me no quiet space. It made me think again about our arrangement, working all day cleaning and washing dishes and waitressing and driving – not at all what I'd signed up for. And then he admitted to me how much he needed the business, to pay off some colossal bills due at the end of the season. I was furious with him for not telling me about them. It meant that however hard we worked, most of the profits were already spent, which affected our arrangement for the end of the season; we'd always be running to catch up. As we talked, details emerged that made me very uncomfortable.

'How could you not tell me from the beginning?'

'But if I'd told you, you wouldn't have come back.'

'Do you think that was fair to me?'

More than anything else, I didn't like dishonesty. It also worried me that he'd got himself in this position, and what it said about him. Being someone generally cautious with money, could I handle this constant uncertainty? At the very least, it was a disorienting shifting of the goalposts.

Needing time to think, I decided to investigate the little house, the *spitaki*. Scooter had been sleeping there but now he had gone. It was a basic concrete hut with a window and a door, and a fireplace in one corner, and was packed full of crates of old taverna paraphernalia, a damp mattress scattered with mouse droppings. But it had potential, and I realised that if I was going to stay, I at least wanted somewhere quiet to escape to when things got chaotic.

For now, I retreated to the tent and fell into a deep and necessary sleep.

Over coffee in the morning, Minas told me how much he appreciated me, we talked things over and I felt better. We calmly and happily got on with our work, and he painted a new sign for the beach advertising the live music. I suggested we promote it as 'Lunch and Live Music', encouraging people to eat with us during the show, and Minas loved the idea. Mid-morning, we heard the familiar and comforting shout of Stamatis coming up from his boat carrying a basket of fish. I paid him from the cash drawer while Minas smashed up a frozen bottle of water with a hammer and packed the fish in a box of ice. Stamatis, barefoot in board shorts and T-shirt, and exhausted from being up since dawn bringing in the nets, lay down on the bench for a nap before driving up to the village to sell the rest of the fish.

'Evgenia!' he shouted from where he was lying. 'Can I have a coffee? Very weak and very sweet.'

'Evgenia! Who's camping on the beach?'

'Evgenia!' he shouted a little later. 'Is everything OK with you?'

I told him about the previous day and Minas having kept things from me. Stamatis reassured me, saying Minas was a good guy really, just a little crazy. I believed he was a good guy, because people in the village liked him, and I trusted their judgement; they just said he was too clever for his own good sometimes, should be more sensible. I'd keep an open mind for now, I thought, and see how things went from here.

I appreciated a quiet day. We only had a couple of tables but they ate well and we didn't miss Scooter's help. I even got some of my own work done and had a swim. Then, in the early evening, Minas received a call from some campers who came most years: ten of them were arriving with guitars in a week's time. He was excited. I walked down to the beach as the colours were fading and the moon rising. A wild wind was blowing through the olives and pine trees, and for a night at least, we had the whole magical valley to ourselves again.

Our first Lunch and Live Music Saturday arrived. The outdoor shower had been painted white and cleaned up ready for guests who wished to wash off the salt of the sea. The rest of the roof was up so people could sit comfortably in the shade, the wooden slats letting through thin stripes of sunshine. One wooden wall at the back was complete and the wind that blew through from the corner had been blocked off temporarily with a stack of green Mythos crates. A few windows had been installed to keep out the dust, without detracting from the feeling of sitting in an olive grove by the sea with hills all around. Stamatis had brought some old tables and chairs; we'd ordered new tops from the carpenter and Minas had painted them. Stamatis had also brought us some beautiful fresh fish.

Tim arrived wearing a white Panama hat, white T-shirt and shorts, bringing tobacco for Minas and carrying a thick songbook. Alison had thoughtfully brought a necklace for me. Captain Nikos had brought people for the show and with others lured by the sign on the beach, some in bathing suits and towels, by lunchtime the restaurant was mildly busy. Lisa, tied in a shady spot under a tree so she couldn't come in and beg from tables, greeted guests as they walked up from the beach, wagging her tail and, if they were appreciative, rolling on to her back for a belly-rub. She, too, was an essential member of the team. As the music began, she barked.

I took orders and brought out carafe after carafe of cold white wine, baskets of fresh bread and olive oil. If people were interested, I carried out the box of fish to show them, let them choose which they wanted, then went inside to weigh and price it accordingly. In between songs, Minas barbecued fish and pork chops and whole calamari stuffed with tomato and cheese. This was what he loved: cooking and making music with friends. I fried potatoes and cut salads and plated up tzatziki with a drizzle of olive oil. I enjoyed the atmosphere, bringing prompt service and my own goofy humour and smiles, taking away empty plates and making coffees and pouring raki. Toned and tanned, I was comfortable in beachwear and loving it. At one point an Italian woman, clearly having a fine time, stood up to perform opera. Her friend covered his ears in jest but everyone else clapped in awe.

I barely had time to hear the music – snippets of 'A Hard Day's Night', 'Brown-Eyed Girl' and, of course, 'Simple Man'. I heard cheers and applause and laughter. And then it was over, and everyone was leaving. It had been a success, and Tim agreed to be back every Saturday.

❖ ❖ ❖ ❖

Ah, going for a dip in the *pisina*, the swimming pool… Slang for doing the dishes in a big, deep restaurant sink. Not very glamorous – the detritus of all that delicious food – and yet it could be satisfying clearing a huge stack of plates, especially when the takings had made it worthwhile, and I could walk outside into sunshine, the blue sea glittering through the trees, my real swimming pool.

Scrubbing down the taverna on a bright, breezy morning could be especially relaxing when I had the place to myself and could do things at my own pace. Minas had driven to town to pick up supplies, and Lisa stood in the field looking up at the road, watching for him. She'd had a wonderful breakfast of lamb chop bones and chips. Leftovers of meat and cheese were always put into the old yoghurt container marked 'Lisa'.

Minas returned just as people began arriving for lunch, and we unloaded the Lada as quickly as possible into the kitchen: Greek coffee, olives, fruit and vegetables and meat, a five-kilo tub of yoghurt (another bucket to add to the collection later), a tray of eggs, a dozen crates of beer and soft drinks. Unfortunately, just as he was reaching in the back of the Lada for the last crate of beer, he knocked the stick that held up the back door and it fell on his head. If he was hurt, he didn't say so; we had both reached a point where you just got on with things. There was continual business all afternoon and we handled it well together, but I cut my finger on the mandolin, slicing potatoes, and I fell over and bruised my knee on the step, an indication of just how tired I was without realising it. The adrenalin kept me going and we didn't stop until 8pm, when I jumped in the sea for a swim as the evening tinged the bay with ruby and grey.

Stamatis joined us for dinner, with his helper Sergei who came from Eastern Europe.

'*Valeh ena raki*,' said Sergei, pointing to his glass. I topped it up.

The meltemi wind was blowing fiercely down from the ridge at the top of the valley, probably funnelled down the gap between the mountains, giving the beach a raw beauty. Karpathos, more exposed than Tilos in an open stretch of the Aegean Sea, was once called Anemoessa, 'The Windy', and Minas had chosen *anemos*, one of the Greek words for wind, as the name of the hotel and taverna. Now I understood why. My tent had been new at the start of the summer, but already the fabric was flimsy and brittle, scorched by the sun and battered by relentless gusts. We placed an online order for a new, bigger one – plus one for Stamatis, and a spare as a 'guest bedroom'. Still, even a big hole in my tent didn't stop me sleeping. And the wind kept mosquitoes away, even in July.

The wind also made simple things like making a phone call or taking a shower more difficult. The outside shower was upwind of the taverna, so clothes and towel were always in danger of being blown away; even the water flow from the shower head would be blown aside, making it challenging to stand under the stream. My long hair started turning to salty blonde dreadlocks.

We had recently replaced the water pump, and just when it seemed that everything at the taverna was working properly, the filter broke – something else that would need replacing. When Minas wasn't fixing something, he often played computer games on his tablet, laughing when the bad guys popped up saying, 'The only option is death!' It did seem sometimes that his troubles popped up with the same regularity, and I imagined them saying, 'The only option is debt.' Whenever I thought we were on top of things, another cost came up. The regulations for running a taverna even in the middle of nowhere were surprisingly specific – we needed a sink for washing hands, a separate sink for cleaning fish, a sink for plates, everything stainless steel.

Making people happy with food continued to fulfil Minas, though, and while cooking he'd say, 'This is going to be the best meal they've ever eaten.' It seemed frankly a tall order and I wondered why he set expectations so high – he felt he had underperformed if the plates weren't all licked clean. I realised later it was like an athlete convincing himself he could win a race. It was positive self-talk.

When people left, he'd say, 'They loved the food, they're definitely coming back tomorrow.' They'd had a good meal, I'd try to explain, but I reckoned they'd probably go somewhere else tomorrow because they were staying far away and wouldn't want to drive here every day. And people like to try new places when they're on holiday. Maybe my taking everything literally and seriously didn't really help. I just didn't like to see him disappointed; it didn't seem healthy the way he would build up his hopes only to have them dashed. He could never understand how people could drive to the beach and not want to come and eat. He wasn't a beach person. He'd prepare based on how many cars had driven down and parked.

Greek people often did like to have a meal and eat well when they went to a beach. It was seen as the right thing to do. So as more Greek people arrived – they usually took their holidays in July and August – we had plenty of late afternoon tables. Whereas a couple from Germany might just order salads, a Greek couple would usually want their table heaped with fish and mezes as well as fried potatoes and a salad they merely picked at.

As a northern European, I was accustomed to enjoying a drink while waiting for the food to be ready, but Greek people would often specify when they placed their order: 'The beer together with the food.' The Greek habit of needing food to go with a drink was good for business as they would always order mezes; groups of Greek men were very good customers; they didn't just drink but prided themselves on eating the best food, and plenty of it. Austrian and Dutch visitors, on the other hand, generally ordered more beers – even better for us as there was no washing up – and we'd give them homemade crisps on the house.

For mezes, Minas prepared tzatziki and *melitzanosalata*, roasted aubergine salad with garlic and red pepper. He created a spectacular version of *saganaki*, fried cheese, with tomato and courgette and olives, all slightly browned and covered in the pan until the cheese began to ooze and the vegetables released their juices, and served with a garnish of fresh basil. When he attempted a new recipe, he'd say, 'No guarantee,' but when it turned out a success he'd add it to the menu.

The cheese was a manouri, a smooth and mild white cheese that came from one of the other mountain villages. A couple of men had come for lunch one day after spearfishing in the bay. One mentioned that he made olivewood charcoal, and his mother made goats' cheese, and we asked for samples next time he came. The cheese was in small, firm rounds and we ordered as much as he could supply, as well as some bags of charcoal, which was more expensive than the supermarket stuff but burned much better.

Although Minas hadn't stopped worrying about money, some busy afternoons we laughed at how well it was going – all the people, the excitement when people saw the fresh fish, the compliments about the food. Despite the constant work, I derived satisfaction too from being part of something *good* that made people happy. It was about doing this as a team, building something together.

Still, there were tense moments. Minas had many strengths, but not chief among them was encouraging and motivating the people who worked for him. I probably had more experience of that from my previous jobs. He didn't realise how stressful it could be answering the phone in the noisiest part of the kitchen, where two fridges and a freezer were labouring away, and taking a room booking in Greek when I could hardly even hear the person.

On a very busy day, he said, 'Don't put plates with food on them into the sink.'

What? I looked around to confirm. 'But there's nowhere else to put them.'

All the work surfaces were stacked high with plates, since we didn't have anyone washing up while we were serving. The sink was the only place.

With such limited resources, we couldn't do things perfectly – and he was just as guilty of that. I was working so hard, and giving so much, that a careless tone of voice from him, something that sounded insulting or sarcastic, was extremely demoralising. I was sensitive to negative moods. We didn't speak to each other for a few hours after that, but luckily chatting to appreciative customers was a good way to relieve the stress.

We made up when things calmed down after 7pm. But I still had to drive up to the village to prepare a room ready for guests arriving the next day. I quickly dived into the sea while Minas heated up some moussaka in the oven for me. After relaxing, I wasn't in any mood to do late-evening room cleaning and preferred to put it off until early the next morning, but he encouraged me to get it done – and to take the rubbish and pick up more cheese. As I drove up the hill, the moon was full and tinged pale tangerine, the sky bathed in dusky sunset red. I headed first to collect cheese from Vasilis at his creamery underneath a church, where the spine of the mountain fell away into pine forest. As I parked, a dozen black-and-white cats stormed the car, trying to get at a rubbish bag that smelled of fish.

Continuing to the village in the dark, I had to slam on the brakes as goats leapt into the road. We'd started keeping the cleaning equipment and the washed sheets and towels in a cupboard in an unfinished room at the bottom of the hotel, but there were no lights down there and the floor was an obstacle course of rubble, something I wished I could fix. It was ridiculous finding matching sheets and towels in the dark. But I got everything done. As I crossed the square, passing Parthenon on my way back again, someone I knew said I was crazy for driving down to the beach now.

'Crazier than you know,' I said.

I passed Evgenia's restaurant and she stopped me to hand me a bag of green peppers grown by her father. Drained of energy, I hungrily eyed the hazelnuts and almonds she had in a bowl and asked for a handful. She insisted on giving me a cup of them for the journey, and I gobbled them up greedily as I drove back along the winding road, with wonderful views of a full, bright moon and the shimmering silver sea below.

Back at the taverna, Minas hadn't made much effort to clean up. I was stroppy, but we had a nightcap together and in the morning he made everything spotless while I swam in the sea, dozed on the beach and ate fresh figs from the tree. He put up the rest of the wood in the corner of the terrace to protect it from the cool evening wind, and that night it came in useful as we hosted a dozen people: Greek campers, Danish visitors, local musicians and fishermen – all drinking raki and eating mezes. Lisa nosed happily around, hoping for fallen scraps.

❖ ❖ ❖ ❖

The third Saturday in July would be one of the busiest days of summer. Captain Nikos called Minas to say he was bringing thirty people for Lunch and Live Music, and we knew there would be plenty of others at the beach. So it was not a good day to wake up and discover the water tank was empty.

Minas had never really explained it to me in full, but water was piped down to the valley from the mountain and because the flow was haphazard, we had a large storage tank. When there was sufficient pressure in the pipes, it filled up our reserve tank, to be pumped and filtered as needed to our kitchen taps, shower, toilet and ice machine. Having an empty tank was not good at any time, but especially not when expecting a lot of guests. I wondered why Minas didn't check the water level regularly. Whether the problem was a blockage or a leak in the pipes, he needed to get the water flowing again somehow. He called the village plumber, but he wasn't available as he had to drive the bus and our water supply was less of a priority.

So Minas, refrigeration engineer and general fixer of broken things, called Vasilis, our cheese-and-honey man who happened to be a retired plumber, then put some tools in the Lada and went in search of the problem. I would have to hold the fort for the morning, doing the cleaning from the night before and a few breakfasts – with hardly any water. Thankfully we had bottles.

The phone rang as I was making an omelette for one of the campers. It was Minas, though I could hardly hear him because of the wind blowing wherever he was on the mountain and the whirring of the fridges and freezer.

'Evgenia, can you check the water filter?'

It might have helped if he'd shown me the system before, or at least briefed me quickly before leaving.

'What am I supposed to check? What am I looking for?' Because we had no mobile signal, I had to put down the phone, go outside and around the back behind the shower, take a look at some unfamiliar equipment and try to identify what he meant. It wasn't at all obvious so I went back and asked.

'Just listen to the water filter and let me know if you can hear it flowing.'

Could I hear a sound coming from somewhere around the water filter? I wasn't sure.

I finished off the breakfasts and in late morning more people started arriving wanting drinks and snacks. I had to explain that the toilet was currently out of order but would be working later, and that I was serving a limited menu until Minas, the chef, arrived. I didn't want to say outright that we had no water as it might put people off coming for lunch. Eventually he called again to say he thought he'd managed to get a bit of water flowing, though he'd injured his back after sliding down a section of the mountain while hauling heavy pipes wearing kitchen slip-ons on his feet.

At least he was on his way. Every time I went into the kitchen to bring out a tray of drinks or mezes, there was another full table, or people walking up from the beach. Smile and wave! I had a semi-hysterical grin on my face when Tim and Alison asked how I was. But I let everyone know Minas was coming soon, and when I saw the Lada I breathed a sigh of relief. He disappeared to the shower to get cleaned up, and when he appeared again he was limping. We checked the taps were working and removed the 'Out of Order' sign from the bathroom.

As the food orders came in, the work was manic. There was no system in the kitchen for me as waitress to post the orders to the chef. He usually simply asked me what the main meal orders were, and kept them in his head, while I took care of everything else. But that day Minas kept asking me what he still needed to make. I was trying to keep my own to-do list in my head while people called out for food and drinks from about a dozen unnumbered tables. We'd never before had a situation where the restaurant was full and everyone clamouring to eat at once.

I preferred to work through orders methodically and tick them off. There was no need to panic; people would get their food as we worked through the orders, they'd understand. Minas, on the other hand, believed it was more efficient to make seven salads at once, although there wasn't space in the kitchen to do that easily – and Italians often wanted their salad without cucumber, some wanted it without cheese, others without onion. Stressed, he demanded I tell him what he still needed to make. I didn't know, and as he became more stressed, my fingers wouldn't work to flip through the order book. The orders started looking blurry. I blinked and swallowed. Tiredness wasn't helping. I tried to stay calm and smiling, which for me was the best way to cope.

Then Captain Nikos came into the kitchen to help.

Of course, it wasn't at all helpful. He criticised Minas for the way he was making something, saying, 'You should have done it like this instead.' Minas then passed along his bad mood to me. We worked much more smoothly when it was just the two of us. Nikos, perhaps stressed about making sure all his customers would eat in time for the boat back, was physically getting in the way, telling us what to do; everyone was tense and snappy and confusion reigned. I had to take some deep breaths, so I walked outside and made a fast loop around the outside of the building to re-set and calm down.

When I came back, they were both still angry, and I couldn't help it – tears started to fall. I really hadn't signed up for this. It wasn't my fault that things were chaotic. So when Nikos started ordering me around, I told him politely but clearly to leave me alone.

'Stop crying, there's work to do!' he said, as if I hadn't noticed, as if I didn't help run this place every single day.

Without thinking or choosing my words, I screamed at him. It wasn't polite this time but seemed to make the point more clearly. I don't think anyone had ever shouted at him that way before. I was a little embarrassed, but it worked. He got out of the kitchen, and I went back to steadily serving the customers. When I took out the next tray, I got some raised eyebrows – but my smile was genuine as I became all sweetness and light again, putting carafes of white wine and plates of food on to tables and asking people, 'Is everything OK?'

Everyone was in good humour, the food and the music and the drinks went down well, and Minas and I went back to working well together as he finished off food orders in between performing songs. The takings were beyond anything we'd seen so far, and we got a few more tables into the evening. Minas would have to drive to town for supplies in the morning.

I later suggested to Minas we needed a system of taping every order to the chef's workstation so he could see clearly what he needed to do, and a number system for the tables. He agreed.

Kapetanios continued to bring boatloads of guests every Saturday for the rest of the summer. But he never came back into the kitchen; and he never spoke to me again.

NEW ARRIVALS

Lifting the fresh bread rolls out of the oven, I couldn't resist tearing one open to release the delicious steam and devouring it while it was still hot – just to test the batch, of course. And it made sense to eat when I could. One busy day, I consumed nothing all day except bread and booze: a glass of wine or a shot of raki with customers gave me energy to keep going. On the go from 8am to 8pm, nothing tasted as good afterwards as an ice-cold Fix beer, straight from the bottle – and I needed the calories.

When everyone left, I'd have a swim, then make myself something to eat. While I liked helping myself to a meal from a taverna kitchen, I usually wanted something quick and simple: just tomatoes and cheese, or fried potatoes with tzatziki, a crêpe loaded with our apple and cinnamon compote and thick cream. I love fresh, natural food and don't like it messed with too much, which probably means I wouldn't make a good chef. Minas, meanwhile, would see a perfectly good chicken breast or calamari and think up a complicated way of stuffing it. And that is what you need to do when you cook for a restaurant.

One of the things that had attracted me to helping at the taverna was the opportunity to learn more about preparing local, seasonal food. Many of the visitors to the beach were looking for that kind of food too. But what I didn't know, and Minas did because he'd been doing it for years, was that in the middle of summer a fair few Italian visitors would want club sandwiches with fries, and Greek campers would want an American quarter-pounder cheeseburger with ketchup and mayo. It drove me crazy that the campers could spend fifteen minutes talking about club sandwiches, but it was probably exotic for them to find authentic American food on an island deep in the Aegean. We needed to offer both.

The big group of campers arrived from Athens and set up their tents discreetly in sheltered gaps in the dense trees at the back of the beach. They were professionals who wanted to have a long holiday and eat well, had been coming for years and loved Minas. Some of them were parents of young children, which meant that mornings involved not only cleaning, making coffees and breakfast – omelettes and toasted sandwiches, yoghurt and honey and fruit – but also trying to entertain a one-year-old who merrily toddled around but often fell over. I preferred to keep an eye on him and distract him than listen to him crying, and I was terrified he was going to injure himself, especially as he liked to follow his mother into our kitchen where she was boiling water for his food.

Minas missed all this, away buying supplies in town, going to several different shops and sometimes the bank, all of which he insisted was worse though I wasn't so sure. However many lighters we bought, he always seemed to take the last one with him to light his cigarettes on the drive, and I had to scramble around to find a way to light the gas burners and oven. It was a little nerve-wracking on days when he was late returning and people were already arriving for lunch; I didn't want to turn customers away but neither did I want to promise they'd be eating within the hour. Minas would ring me once he was on his way, and when he arrived we'd quickly unload the Lada and find space for things in the fridges. He'd turn up the music, perhaps to drown out the rest of the mayhem.

When we had people at the rooms, one set of guests leaving around midday and another set arriving two hours later, after holding the fort all morning I'd take the trusty Lada and dash up to the village. I'd hurry through the alley to do the changeover in time – laundry, drying, ironing, cleaning – then call out greetings to everyone in the village as I dashed back down to the taverna, where things often got a little loud and frenzied in late afternoon.

The campers said, 'You must have such a lovely, easy, quiet life here.' I was so tired I could cry, but I laughed instead.

Another signal that the full summer season was finally upon us was that we'd be offering ice cream. In preparation, Minas had set up an extra freezer in the corner of the terrace, and already people were coming up from the beach to ask for ice cream, only to be disappointed to find we didn't yet have any. Finally, the day arrived when the supplier was coming up to the north of the island in the refrigerated truck. Of course, they refused to come down our bumpy, winding track, so Minas – who'd perfected this system over several years – drove up to the road in the Lada, collected the ice creams, and hurtled back down at top speed before they melted.

And now it was full season, on busy days we might take a lot of cash. Not making money had been stressful, of course, but making money could be stressful too, as at that point we didn't have a safe, so we would have to hide it somewhere. Minas had entrusted that part to me: keeping the accounts and hiding the money.

One early evening, after Minas had picked up our new tents from the post office in town, I was looking forward to a leisurely break pitching mine. But the moment I started, the campers came over and weighed in with their opinions of where and how to do it. I tried explaining that I knew how to put a simple dome tent up, I'd been putting up tents since I was a teenager and had been sleeping in one for months. But how could an English person know how to put up a tent? Besides, they were enjoying themselves and only wanted to help, and I didn't have the energy to fight it. Once they started grabbing the poles and flysheet, I left them to it and walked down to the beach.

Later on, they joined several tables together and sat around playing guitars and singing. I knew I should join them but was finding it difficult to switch off and be comfortable with people around all the time. I'd come here partly because I liked remote and lonely places. I was also anxious, concentrating on getting things right. It was still July and already I couldn't wait for things to calm down, for no talking, no music. I walked out into the field under a beautiful dark sky and followed the path to the beach, where the only sound was the sea as it played with the shoreline.

Every morning now, I'd hope there wasn't already a queue for the bathroom. More campers were arriving from the city, further extending our working day. We put on the hot water, sluiced down and mopped the kitchen and bathroom, made coffees, washed up, made breakfast and bread, did more washing up; tiring work, non-stop for several hours, but at least we didn't have to talk to anyone while bent over the sink with the radio on. One morning, one of the campers told me Minas had to make her coffee as he made it better than I did. What enviable people skills, I thought, offended and grumpy. Still, I felt enormously glad not to be a person whose day could be ruined by an imperfect coffee. Thankfully, a Polish couple made up for it later when they asked me for a frappe coffee with ice cream, then said it was the best they'd had on the island and left a two-euro tip. I made myself one, thinking it would be a good energy boost, then didn't have time to drink it until it was melted and warm.

I'd somehow expected the campers to be relaxed, laid-back people; that belief was further debunked as it seemed they were constantly shouting for something. They were a group of friends reunited in a familiar summer home. *Give me this, give me that. Not like this, like that. Relax, take your time Jen – but where is my tzatziki? And Minas, make fish soup!* Stamatis had given the campers fish for soup and everyone insisted that Minas should make it. Preparing Greek *psarosoupa* is a strict and complex process and everyone had an opinion about how to do it right – for them, that was part of the fun as they took over the kitchen. It gave me a big headache, but Minas loved being in full work mode, running around making all sorts of different things to keep his friends happy.

'I can make money out of thin air with food,' said Minas. And he could. One evening, none of the campers had ordered food, but when he cooked spaghetti with chicken and garlic in fresh tomato sauce, the aroma made one of them hungry, and once that person ordered a plate and everyone else saw it, they all wanted some. Then he made crêpes with strawberry compote and cream, drizzled with chocolate, and everyone wanted those too.

Nursing a headache again, I sat quietly and made a calendar for the hotel rooms, sticking it on the wall by the phone so we could see at a glance what was available when, and could also see in advance when I'd need a few hours in the village. At least my organisational skills behind the scenes helped things run more smoothly. I made myself something to eat and hoped to get a good night's sleep. I knew that if I wasn't so tired, I'd enjoy things more.

My feet and back had been hurting for a while, and that night I had a sudden flash of inspiration: I needed better shoes. Since the weather had become far too hot for boots, I'd been working twelve-hour days wearing flat leather sandals with no support in them at all. I mentioned this to Minas and he realised his back was hurting too. I hadn't been to town for months and wouldn't have chance for the foreseeable future, so I added training shoes to his shopping list. Having a running shopping list was another organisational innovation of mine; next year perhaps, we'd develop a checklist: flour, eggs, yoghurt, bacon, tomatoes, onions, peppers etc. It would be easier not having to remember everything.

Yes, next year: however hard this was, however upsetting it could be at times, I still hoped that I'd be here next year; we'd just do things better. All this – Minas, the beach, the village – they were all strangely turning into home.

Minas encouraged me to go for a swim at midday as it might subtly alert potential customers to our whereabouts. I lay on the warm, smooth, flat pebbles at the water's edge, noticing how it transformed them from pale grey to purple, brown and white. The sea varied from blue to emerald green and was often so clear I could see every pebble on the smooth seabed as I swam. While throwing sticks into the water for Lisa, I met a Dutch family with a teenage girl who loved dogs and asked to join in. They came up for lunch and became regular customers, partly to visit Lisa.

Meanwhile, the neighbours had come back and gradually opened their taverna. Whenever I passed it on my drive up to the village, they looked daggers at me. So although the weather was gorgeous in the valley as August began, sunny with a light breeze, the beach didn't feel quite as relaxed with someone sitting all day by the big white shipping container and steering people to the other taverna. The woman once tried saying nasty things about Minas to me, and I'd heard she did the same to others. Minas explained that one reason he'd been so anxious to remodel the kitchen according to the regulations and get a full licence was because otherwise the neighbours could call the council and get him closed down. Hostility seemed so sad and pointless.

No-one wanted to be hassled by touts on a beach like ours. But this was the silly season.

Each day when I drove up to Olympos there were more cars, and I had to park the Lada further and further away from the village. A local man shouted at me for blocking access and I had to squeeze past tour groups on the crowded alley, waving and smiling at people. When I reached Uncle Nick's one day, he was yelling at his waitress (though she didn't look scared – she was bigger than him and yelling back); another day there was broken glass in the alley just outside his taverna and I was shocked to hear that something had been thrown through a window. The waitress stood on the balcony shouting at passers-by to come inside, her job being to divert people's attention from other restaurants, even ones owned by family members. It might not be obvious to outsiders, but on every Greek island, tempers become frayed in the height of summer, resulting in everything from fights to lawsuits.

I saw how for Minas just the loan payments and the electricity and maintenance added up to a lot, never mind anything else. It was difficult being caught up in the worries of how much business we had and what we could do about it. I realised how stressful it was for people who relied on their summer business to get through the winter; I was lucky to have my other work that I could do from anywhere (except, it seemed, a taverna by the sea…). If he had a bad summer, Minas could work in Athens for the winter, living in his family's house in Piraeus, but he hoped to stay here on Karpathos. And I hoped I could too.

One day, I didn't have to clean a hotel room at midday so we handled lunch together at the taverna and then I drove up to the village later. The wind was so strong – especially on our side of the village, on the west side of the mountain high above the coast – that it was a challenge to peg clean sheets on the line, after which they flapped damply in the mist. On my list of things to do was pick up the signs we'd ordered from the carpenter's workshop, but I was so late that the shop was closed; thankfully they had been left outside for me. On the drive back, I made a quick detour to Vasilis for cheese and honey as a spectacular sunset infused the pale rock and cloud with colour. Minas's aunt Sophia was there and gave me a pack of Marlboros for him that she'd been carrying in the hem of her skirt. I talked with her and stroked her dog while waiting for Vasilis to feed the goats. Finally heading off down the hill in the Lada, I was forced to slow down when I found myself stuck behind two of the campers, and felt like an impatient local.

My relief to be home was mitigated by seeing that Minas had made a huge mess in the kitchen, his eyes glazed with booze; it probably wasn't surprising, when he had had to handle the afternoon without any help. But he had also baked me some cheese with tomato and pepper wrapped in foil over the charcoal, and it was delightful. I poured myself a little carafe of wine and enjoyed the luxury of reading a book while the campers drank carafes of raki, playing music, and Minas watched football on my laptop. The cool wind was a blessing. Lisa started whining, perhaps wanting to join us in the taverna, or perhaps wanting to chase goats. Unfortunately, when tied up she had no inclination to keep them away and a skinny old goat that had been wandering around for days had eaten half the courgette plants we'd been growing.

Stamatis and Sergei arrived for the evening, Sergei cajoling me to find him a girlfriend in England and intermittently demanding another glass of raki. I went inside to grab the bottle from the freezer, and noticed the drains were smelling bad. I hoped they would survive another few weeks.

'Thanks for being part of my crazy summer,' said Minas.

The campers stayed up late that evening, so again I wandered beyond the lights into the dark fields and looked up at the Milky Way, the *galaxia*. I decided I'd take a sleeping bag and pillow down to the beach and lie there for a while, to rest in comfort and listen to the sea. I woke up hours later on the silent shore.

❖ ❖ ❖ ❖

And then, one afternoon, we saw a bulldozer coming down the track. A team of men working for the neighbours dug two rows of holes, filled them with cement and stuck in metal poles for beach umbrellas. I felt sick, grief-stricken for the pristine, natural beach.

The campers agreed that it was all wrong, especially in a conservation area, and I was glad they were on our team. That evening, I joined the group drinking raki, and got into the spirit of things. Sitting together as they played Greek songs on guitar, the mood felt special and we all got to know one another better. We didn't get to sleep until 3am, but my mood was improved the next day.

'*Chronia polla!*'

Stamatis brought us lots of good fish in late morning. People saw him carrying the fish up the beach and would follow to have a closer look. The sight of red snapper, sea bream and red mullet pulled from the net that morning often enticed people to treat themselves to a special lunch. It always helped us to have a good day; he was such an important part of the taverna.

Minas returned from town with a pair of new trainers for me which were perfect – white and silver, they fit snugly and I felt instantly better. (Plus, I was impressed: a man who can choose me a pair of shoes…) I also realised that for months I'd been wearing old jean shorts and cheap vest T-shirts, which not only looked scruffy now but felt hot and cumbersome when it was forty degrees in the kitchen. In my backpack, I had a dress I had hoped might be useful when I was packing to come here for the summer: super-short and backless, in camo print, it easily slipped over a bikini. It might be rather risqué but given there was war at the beach, it felt like appropriate ammunition; it was comfortable and fun, and I felt ready for action in my new trainers. Minas did a double-take: he clearly approved.

My hands were full of cuts and burns, I realised. I didn't even remember how they happened. My feet and body felt better now that I was wearing trainers, and to combat the headaches I started making a bigger effort to eat. In the morning I had thick yoghurt and oranges and honey, maybe an egg if the yolk broke in the frying pan while I was frying breakfast for customers, as well as a few figs from the tree.

I made sure I had a quick swim at midday, doing my best to avoid the umbrellas and the neighbour who stalked around in black casting vicious looks at me. My new friends, the campers, would look after the taverna for twenty minutes. Most of our lunch customers were Greek, and I was proud to be able to greet a Greek family and explain the menu to them in their language, and even make their Greek salad. A French-Chinese couple bought a big sea bream and wanted it with vegetables, so Minas grilled courgette slices, slightly charred with garlic and sprinkled with oregano. It was so good, we put grilled courgettes on the menu as a new meze. While the charcoal was hot, he grilled me a couple of red scorpion fish; so called because their spines packed a nasty sting, they were usually reserved for fish soup, but I loved them barbecued. They had to sit on a plate for two hours while we were busy, but even cold they tasted magnificent, the flesh firm and white.

Minas's leg was hurting after a gas tank fell on it, so I wasn't the only one with injuries, or over-tired. When I returned from a beautiful swim at dusk with the wind whipping up the waves, he was slumped in the corner, falling asleep on the cushioned bench.

'Don't let me sleep here all night,' he said. I tried waking him later but he waved me off.

When all the customers and campers had gone and he was sleeping, and it was finally peaceful, I laughed at the whole situation. I turned off the lights and locked the kitchen, blocking off some of the noise from the fridges, then walked to my tent. The Milky Way was a stripe across the starry sky. It was the first night in ages I'd felt so relaxed and calm. My new tent was already semi-destroyed by the constant tugging of the wind and flapped too much to be conducive to sleep, so like Minas I found myself a cushioned bench and got into my sleeping bag, looking at the stars above. I envisioned waking up there in the winter, when no-one else was around.

Rested from a good sleep, I left Minas to do cleaning therapy – which now included changing the oil in the deep-fat fryer because it was getting so much use and took all morning – and make breakfasts while I drove up to Olympos to clean a room. My new trainers turned out to be ideal for running through the village, and most of my village friends were busy talking to visitors so I just waved cheerily as I dashed along the alley. The guests had locked their key inside their room and we couldn't find the spare, so I climbed over the wall of the balcony to let myself in. I looked after the plants on the balcony, picking off dead leaves and watering everything, propping open the doors carefully using wooden jambs so they didn't slam shut. After sweeping the balcony and room, I went outside to empty the dustpan and a sudden gust of wind blew all the dust and leaves out again, half into my face and the rest all over the floor. I swept it again and emptied the dustpan more carefully.

Finished at last, I carried a big bag of rubbish to the bins near where I'd parked. I was also hefting a bag full of wet laundry – our clothes and towels, since the washing machine at the taverna wasn't working – and five litres of olive oil from the barrel. As if my bags weren't heavy enough, I also squeezed in some boxes of extra knives and forks from storage, because we'd been running low on cutlery on the busy days, not having any help to wash things as they came back to the kitchen. It was a mad physical challenge, carrying all that and dodging coach parties of tourists, feeling like a donkey. Now a donkey would be useful, I thought.

'Do you never eat? You've lost so much weight!' said one of the shop owners along the alleyway.

Minas's aunt Sophia needed a ride down to the valley to chase her goats off the olive trees; they became more aggressive about finding things to eat as the summer wore on, the relentless sun drying out all the vegetation. Sophia helped her daughter Evgenia run her restaurant in Olympos, and in August they didn't always have time to round up the goats. Sophia came to meet me at the Lada, wearing her traditional leather boots and dress, her black sleeves rolled up to reveal arms strong from working with animals – and carrying a couple of ice-cream sandwiches, one for me. She soon had me laughing and chatting about the tribulations of dealing with men, much more therapeutic than the time alone would have been. Reminding me I was welcome at their place whenever I had time, she insisted on being dropped off on the hillside, and strode off across country.

I arrived back to find that once again there was no water. Minas was stressed and had lost a couple of customers due to having to deal with the crisis, but now I was back he got stuck into fixing the problem. Of course, because of that he hadn't replenished the supply of bread for dinner, so I had to start kneading dough right away. This time he was better prepared to fix the water problem and got back in time to deal with some late afternoon customers. The mood was relaxed and happy, people complimenting us on the food and reminding us that we lived in paradise.

Most of the campers were gradually coming to feel like friends as the weeks went by. Fondas and Alex were always trying to help and inject humour into things. I'd relaxed somewhat with them, realising what an important part of the beach community they were, supporting Minas and other local businesses over the years and looking after the place. They'd also realised that I wasn't just someone who arrived for a job but had invested a lot in the business for my own reasons, and still had to do my other work. After we ate, Minas sat singing while two of the campers played guitar. At first I had bristled at the campers walking into the kitchen and helping themselves, but now I was grateful that I didn't have to get up every time someone wanted something. They preferred looking after themselves and feeling at home, not waiting to be served. They'd take what they needed and tell me, 'Jen – one Cornetto! Jen – one water!'

I started a system of taping everyone's tab to the kitchen wall so they could add what they'd taken, and most of them liked to settle up every morning after breakfast so there was no confusion and they knew what they were spending, without having to carry money around. We offered reduced 'camper' prices for certain things, since they were often with us for weeks, and gave out free carafes of raki from time to time. When Minas went shopping in town, they give him a list of things they needed – usually fruit and tobacco. I started to enjoy making breakfasts – it gave me an opportunity to be a little creative in the kitchen, albeit in a simple way: omelette with green pepper and feta and mushrooms and bacon, cheese and bacon toasties with tomato... Someone loved my scrambled eggs and Alex always made me laugh when he asked for 'eggs eyes', the literal translation of the Greek phrase for 'sunny side up'. It got to the point where I was reluctant to hand over the orders to Minas and drive up to the village.

One day, on my drive back down to the beach, I was tired and my mind was meandering as much as the track itself when I met another car on a blind turn and had to brake sharply. I had to reverse uphill to the nearest passing place – easier said than done, since we were already almost bumper to bumper and the Lada didn't have a properly functioning handbrake. The driver gave me a very dirty look. As I continued downhill, shaken, the driver's seat inched forward as usual. Minas had tried fixing the seat before I left, but by the time I reached the valley, my knees were on the steering wheel and, dangerously, I could barely work the pedals.

'Why does nothing work properly around here?' I asked him, exasperated and a little upset.

It made him feel bad to hear it, perhaps especially because he knew it was true. But he was already in the midst of a big debate about the neighbours with one of the campers, Theresa. Minas had decided to call the police and lodge a complaint about the beach umbrellas and the neighbour leading people to her taverna, both of which were illegal. He was concerned about losing business, not just now but in the long term, afraid that the umbrellas and the hassle would drive away the people who came here to get away from all that. A customer had told me she'd even shouted at him angrily for turning his sunbed around. It wouldn't take much to stop people driving down that road.

Theresa, who was an artist and had built her shelter on the beach out of driftwood, was by no means a fan of the umbrellas. What's more, she and her partner had seen a turtle lay eggs on the beach a few years back. They felt very privileged to have seen it, and Stamatis had told them he saw turtles around here too. It made the planting of permanent concrete bases for umbrellas deep in the beach even less acceptable. But Theresa also worried that if the police were called they would fine the campers because free camping was, though accepted, technically illegal. She was afraid to lose what they had.

And Minas couldn't afford to risk losing the campers either – they were important customers as well as friends. We also had returning customers, the people who came for the music days and the guests staying in our rooms, who usually came to the taverna at least for a visit, but fewer and fewer casual visitors to the beach were slipping through the neighbours' net.

The discussion became louder, and Minas turned the music right up. He told me how much he appreciated my sticking around through the mayhem, then fell asleep on the bench. With things calmer, I gradually turned down the music and got on with my evening. But a new group of campers arrived late from the ferry and wanted to eat. I explained the owner was asleep but I could make them salads and fried potatoes and burgers, and they were all happy with that. Fondas, playing backgammon with Theresa, offered to light the barbecue if they wanted fish, but I decided they could have fish tomorrow. For once, I was the one relieved to see clean plates as they ate everything I gave them. Other campers gathered for drinks and, feeling confident and happy, I made them a few plates of mezes to go with the raki. It was fun having free rein in the kitchen.

The next morning Minas was still determined to lodge a complaint and was convinced the police would charge down to investigate immediately. I hoped they wouldn't. I was fairly convinced they would have other things to do, anyway. Later, though, I wondered if it was possible to report ten campers to the police for sitting around singing 'Yellow Submarine'. *Perhaps it's not actually a crime, but oh, it should be.*

And I could no longer escape to the *spitaki* – because our new helper was there.

SPEEDY GEORGE

For a month in the height of the summer season, Minas and I had been running a taverna and a small hotel in two different locations between the two of us with no other help. It was absurd.

Yet I'd been in favour of us handling it ourselves because we worked well together, and because takings were low and outgoings high. The Scooter experience hadn't been great and had often just added more work and stress. Still, we were both utterly exhausted, with no time off. When our friend Pavlos mentioned he knew someone who was looking for work, we agreed to take him on.

Like Scooter, and like most of the people who do cleaning and labouring jobs in Greece, Safet was Albanian, but had spent years helping in kitchens in Thessaloniki and working the olive harvest in Mytilene, so he used a Greek name, Yorgos. After the friction with Scooter, Minas made it clear from the beginning that I was the second boss. Yorgos was tired from his journey, so Minas told him to settle in and that he could start work the next morning.

And in the morning, we really appreciated him. Things were much easier with a helpful third person, and he anticipated things we needed, doing jobs before we asked, always keeping busy. Slim and dark, in his late forties and married with children, he wore board shorts and T-shirt and trainers, and seemed professional and cheerful. It was lovely for me to have the time to take Lisa for a walk up to the church, and not have to hurry manically when I drove up to the village.

One of our Greek hotel guests earlier in the summer had asked us to post them a receipt after they left, not realising what an ordeal it would be in a place with no post office. I'd hoped they would forget about it but they'd recently enquired again, and I worried they might cause a fuss, so I had a new challenge that day while doing the cleaning and laundry. I wasn't going to send Minas running around town just to find an envelope in the heat and madness of summer when we needed him at the restaurant. The little mini-market in the village of course didn't sell envelopes, but did have coffee and sugar, which I decided to add to the hotel kitchen for guests. Thankfully, when I mentioned my predicament to a man in another shop, he found an envelope and gave it to me for nothing. The villagers were so friendly to me and supportive.

It was always a boost to arrive back at the taverna and see my lovely Lisa wagging her tail. The view of the sea kept me going too, as did meeting good people, I thought as I launched straight into waitressing. A Serbian couple said they loved the seclusion of the beach, the exotic feel of the whole island, and wondered how long it could stay that way. It reinforced what we felt about the umbrellas.

Now that we had Yorgos to help, it was more apparent that although we did have business, the restaurant was often pretty quiet for August. There had been no sign of any police coming to investigate illegal umbrellas or anything else, and our neighbour continued to approach visitors as soon as they arrived. I was tired, feeling that all our efforts were being thwarted, and Minas wasn't in a great mood either. I was doing my best to remain upbeat when he started telling me condescendingly how to fry potatoes. I had made a mistake with one batch, just as he sometimes made mistakes when he left the freezer open or dropped food. I had fried a perfect batch just five minutes earlier, but the criticism made me nervous and more likely to make mistakes. Thankfully, once the guests left, he fell asleep early again on the bench.

I enjoyed a bit of calm and sat in the corner dealing with bookings for the rooms. Because mix-ups had occurred about arrival times and keys and payment methods, I was now trying to send messages in advance to clients, ideally before they left for their trip in case they'd booked using an office email address. Many people didn't realise that there were no banks or petrol stations in this part of the island and were grateful for the advice about what to expect, as well as directions. The system seemed to work as I got immediate confirmation responses. I also started to plan my own work for September.

A couple arrived for food at 10.30pm and I took their order. If we were on the premises, we were open for business. Stamatis cleaned the fish and between us we managed to wake Minas to grill it, then he went back to sleep. It really was a communal effort around here. The wine and the peace and quiet mellowed me and as I got ready for bed, I thought: in spite of my grouchiness sometimes, I had no regrets about this summer. The tent would be flapping in the wind, but I'd sleep well. And now we had Yorgos to do all the cleaning in the morning, and the daily takings would cover his wages, and we'd have fun with nice, friendly people – new friends and old.

And then we woke up yet again to no water at all in the taps or tank.

That's OK, I'll just make my frappe coffee with raki instead.

While Minas went to check the water up the mountain and try to get it flowing, all the campers descended at once for breakfast so I was making coffees and squeezing orange juice and cooking eggs and toasties non-stop, and baking a first batch of bread. Yorgos did all the cleaning efficiently, so I nicknamed him '*o Grigoros*', Speedy George. When Minas returned, there was still no water in the taps but apparently it was flowing into the tank. Then he announced, out of the blue, 'You'd better leave to clean the rooms right away, as we've got thirty people coming for lunch.'

I told him I'd been too busy to make more than one batch of bread, so he'd need to make more.

'OK,' he said in a curt tone, as if I'd done something wrong that he was prepared to overlook. 'Just hurry and get back here as soon as you can.'

I felt like walking out. It was already late morning and I'd have to be superhuman to dash up to the village, clean two rooms and be back in time to help with lunch. I gathered up the bags of rubbish and put them in the back of the car. Fish bones had made holes in the bags, so they leaked into the car, drenching it in stinking liquid – why didn't he have a container to put them in? The car seat was so far forward again I could hardly get in – never mind out, which was bad news in case of an emergency. I tried to move it but couldn't as it was all so rusted. I called Minas to come and sort it out. I could have used an encouraging word or two.

As I drove past the neighbours' taverna, they shouted 'Greetings to Minas!' with an odd sneer. I didn't feel comfortable, didn't understand what they had against us. A hunch told me to drive back and take Lisa with me, scared that something might happen to her. But when I returned to the taverna, Minas told me to leave her. I drove up to the village in tears. All the parking spaces were full and I had to drive back along the road to find somewhere. The village was a madhouse of tour groups and locals heckling, *Come into my restaurant, nice place...* Nice place indeed, I groaned.

A Greek couple had booked one of our rooms for a week. Minas had taken the booking directly ages ago but hadn't noted which room they requested; it turned out they'd specifically wanted the one with the bigger balcony. For now, they were staying in the upstairs room but had asked to move to the lower room as soon as it became available, that morning. So I now had to clean an extra room, the room where they'd been staying – and had no idea where they'd left the key. Minas couldn't find their contact details. He said there was a spare key somewhere in his kitchen, but when I looked there were at least a dozen keys lying around and nothing was labelled.

As I went down to the laundry room to fetch the clean sheets, thinking that with no-one on site at the hotel on a regular basis, surely it would be a good idea to have a key safe system, as well as a clean space for doing laundry in the hotel itself, I banged my head badly on the low doorway. I must be exhausted, I thought, realising that I'd been crying for hours. All the doors of the house had expanded with the damp from the mountain mist, the clouds that flowed over the peak bringing water to the village, and were stiff to open and close – everything was harder than it should be. At that moment, I just wanted the summer to be over. Eventually I took all the keys over to the hotel and was trying them in the lock when someone opened the door.

'Oh hi…' he said sleepily and smiling, just waking up. 'We decided not to change rooms after all. We like it here.'

They'd fallen under the spell of the place, as I had. Grateful for small mercies, I wished them a lovely day, then went downstairs to the lower room to leave it ready. As I made up the bed, I wanted nothing more than to sink down and sleep, in the very bed where I'd decided to take all this on in the first place. Would I be running the hotel next year?

Leaving the village, I bought a large bar of chocolate and ate the whole thing in one go. Sophia at her café saw me and waved, asking if I was OK.

'I think so,' I said.

'*Ipomoni,*' she said. Patience.

It was mid-afternoon when I arrived back to chaos at the taverna. There was still no water, and we had a busy restaurant. Yorgos had been bringing bucketloads of seawater up in order to do the cleaning. I helped out by dealing with a few tables but Minas seemed oblivious, drinking and singing. I went for a swim but it didn't help much. Stamatis saw me and said I seemed unhappy.

'Hang in there if you can,' he said. 'Maybe have a break.'

I took his advice and took Lisa for a walk.

Minas continued to ignore me when I got back, so as the campers started arriving for the evening, knowing he had Yorgos to help him, I went to the tent and fell blissfully asleep. But instead of letting me grab some rest, he woke me up, asking what was wrong. If he'd been more sober, I could have tried to talk to him, though I was probably still too upset for that and too tired to think clearly. I waited for him to go, then took my sleeping bag and pillow and found a dark, quiet spot by the beach, and watched shooting stars. I thought again about leaving. But it wouldn't be fair to him, not in the busiest part of summer; I wouldn't feel good about it. It was only a little while longer until things calmed down. I would miss this place, the beach. And I'd put so much in already. I wanted to make it work. I wanted to stay for the quiet times.

I woke at dawn and had a swim just as the sunlight started to warm the empty beach. There was just Sergei sitting on the fishing boat, cleaning nets.

Well rested, in the calm of morning, I felt strong again. It was a beautiful day, with not a breath of wind. It was approaching the middle of August, when everyone wanted to escape to a beach. It was also the last Lunch and Live Music of the summer and we hoped for a busy day. It was only just after noon when the tables started to fill up. I could only laugh. Speedy George had done the washing up and cleaning with seawater, then he and Minas had gone to try and fix the damaged water pipe properly. They might be gone for some time.

Smile and wave, Minas always said, so I did.

'Hello! Welcome. Sit wherever you like and I'll be with you in a minute.'

At least I could relax and handle things in my own way, at my own pace, smile and joke with customers.

Not only did we not have a chef, we also didn't have a great deal of food, as for days Minas hadn't been able to drive to town for supplies. With every table in the taverna full, I apologised that we had run out of half our stock as we were so busy the day before. Most people didn't mind at all – they were happy to eat and drink whatever we had. Who cared if special omelette and chips wasn't on the lunch menu? I could also make toasted sandwiches and chips, dips and salads. Soon there was a pleasant hum of conversation and a soothing clink of cutlery.

Yorgos returned with good news that the blockage was fixed and water would be flowing soon – Minas still had work to do but sent him back down with a passing car. He efficiently took bread baskets to people and made coffees. We worked together well.

Tim and Alison arrived, and there were kisses all round. I couldn't believe their stay on the island was almost over and I'd barely had time to talk to them. They asked how I was. I smiled and told them about the water problems, but that Minas had been a hero and fixed them. Then, suddenly, there was a strange noise, a kind of... explosion.

I had no idea what it was, until someone pointed to the back of the taverna behind the shower. I ran out to see a jet of water spraying several metres high into the air from the hot water tank. Of course.

I could only guess that the sudden surge of water must have been too much for the old tank. I went to investigate, until one of the campers, Alex, sensibly and kindly mentioned that it was quite close to the electrics, and I was perhaps at risk of electrocution. So, we had a taverna full of people and water spraying high in the air, with a possibility of blowing the electrics or someone being electrocuted. Trying to stay calm, I wondered what I should do. *What do you do when a hot water tank explodes?*

'Which is the fuse for the hot water tank?' Alex asked, again helpfully. I had no idea and it wasn't labelled. The first thing to do was call Minas.

The only way we had of calling out was using Skype on my computer, since Minas hadn't been able to put credit in the taverna phone and I clearly couldn't walk up to the church to get a signal to use my mobile. I tried to ignore the curious looks from customers as, in the midst of lunch service and evident crisis, I calmly sat down to fire up my laptop. There was no answer. That, at least, was a good sign, as if he was out of range, he might be on his way... Sure enough, suddenly I heard the engine of the Lada. He went immediately to take care of the hot water tank, and I carried on making lunches and drinks, totting up bills and clearing tables ready for new customers arriving.

Once things were under control, I told him about how things had gone in his absence. Instead of being pleased that I'd been able to take care of business, he was angry that when we had a full taverna, he hadn't been here to cook fish and other meals that would have brought in more money. This time, I wasn't going to let the negativity bother me: I knew people were satisfied and we'd made it through the crisis.

More people were arriving from the beach and all the tables were full, one couple perched on a wall – we needed to fetch the older tables and chairs to make extra places. I brought drinks for Tim and Alison as they and their friends settled in at the top table and Tim got out his guitar.

The last live music session was as hectic as ever, and soon I was running in and out of the kitchen as people shouted orders for more wine, more beers, more potatoes… People sang along, and danced, ate and drank and had fun. It was exhausting but exhilarating; this was what we were all about. Minas, after his ordeal of the morning, drank a few beers and sang a few songs. Just before the boat left, all at once people started to ask for their bills, and I cleared a space in the kitchen to cut up a huge watermelon for everyone. We just need to get through this last hour and then we could take a break.

And then Minas mentioned that he'd bought a goat – to roast on a spit that afternoon.

After single-handedly serving a full restaurant, a water tank disaster and the biggest live music day of the summer, now we'd be roasting a goat. This day wouldn't end. Of course, it would draw lots of customers.

❖ ❖ ❖ ❖

Roasting a whole goat on the spit turned out to be no mean feat. First, the poor recently slaughtered animal arrived in a bag brought by Vasilis, who'd helped fix the water problem. As the guys carried it into the kitchen to perform the brutal task of running a steel rod through it and securing it at either end, I made myself scarce.

Then the huge spit had to be set up. Powered using a motor borrowed from some other piece of equipment, it made a whirring noise like a very large fly buzzing around a jar over and over. And over and over.

Lisa got as close as her lead would reach and sat transfixed.

Most people reserved their evening meal in advance, at least. As the afternoon turned to early evening, tables started to fill, and people asked excitedly how long it would be before they could eat. Having absolutely no idea, I asked Minas.

'Oh, about forty-five minutes,' he said. I relayed this information to the guests, who ordered carafes of wine, raving about what a beautiful place we had and asking what life was like here. If only they knew.

'Excuse me?' asked a couple an hour or so later. 'Do you know if the goat will be ready soon?'

I checked again with Minas how long it would be.

'About forty-five minutes,' he said with a straight face.

I apologised but the people said it was fine – they were on holiday, no rush and ordered appetisers and salads and more drinks.

After the third 'About another forty-five minutes', I began to get suspicious, and so did everyone else. One young couple, seeing the writing on the wall, decided to accept our offer of the 'guest room' – the spare tent and sleeping bags – and ordered a carafe of raki. They hadn't brought much money with them to the beach, not expecting to be staying for dinner, but Minas said they could settle up another time. A couple from Germany asked if we had more sleeping bags and decided to camp also.

When eventually the goat was ready, some five hours later, it took several men to deal with it – two to carry it into the kitchen and the rest to debate how to portion it up. I squeezed past, trying to take care of the orders outside, and slid across the floor. The kitchen was swimming with grease and bits of meat. Plates were shouted for. In all those hours of 'another forty-five minutes', I'd been given no sense at all of what I needed to prepare or that the cooking was nearly done, and suddenly, instantly, we needed enough potatoes to serve with a whole goat.

But I got potatoes frying and was soon ferrying plates of meat out to people, who started to dig in contentedly. Everyone said the goat was magnificent. We had to take their word for it – there wasn't a morsel left over. People asked for more and more bread until we ran out, and Minas insisted I make another batch even though I knew full well that by the time it was ready everyone would have finished and gone. I was infuriated with him – after the day I'd had. But it was hard to stay angry for long when things had gone so well and the takings would cover our money problems for a while.

Another forty-five minutes – and I'd be fast asleep.

❖ ❖ ❖ ❖

In the height of summer, people were always drifting in and out of the taverna, day and night. The big ferry, the *Prevelis*, arrived at Diafani late and campers would come looking for food or water, and if we were up we'd look after them.

One beautiful late evening, windy and cool, a group of young Greek people arrived to say they'd got their car stuck on a sharp bend in the road and were afraid to move it. They were planning to camp here anyway, but blocking the road in the dark could be dangerous.

Minas was asleep but I was sure he would help. I tried to wake him but he refused to budge. I thought for a moment about what I could do, then tried shaking him again, saying, 'There are customers who need feeding…'

He roused himself, and I explained he had to rescue their stranded car first.

Since our permanent campers were happy to look after themselves late at night, often they'd be talking and drinking just a few metres away from me as I drifted in and out of sleep in my tent in the field.

One night, I woke up with a start, panicking as I realised that I was supposed to be serving a large fish to waiting customers. It took me a while to understand that there wasn't a fish, and I was dreaming. We couldn't even have time off in our sleep.

'I think I need to eat better,' I said to Minas in the morning.

My body didn't seem to be functioning well on a diet of chips and chocolate, which is all I'd got around to eating that week. No-one had stopped me; I just never felt like eating when we were busy serving and clearing other people's plates, and I didn't feel like making food when there was chaos and mess in the kitchen. But because that was most of the day, I tended to keep going without a meal until I was too tired to know what I wanted or go through the process of getting it.

'Also, if I have time for a swim in the sea, it makes me a happier person and therefore a better waitress.'

Minas grinned and said it was hard to argue with that. I was heading off to the beach when Alex asked me to make up his bill for the previous day. Whereas usually I'd have gone ahead and done it right away, and inevitably got caught up in something else and missed my downtime, instead I asked if he could wait until later. And he said sure, no problem.

Lisa didn't want to come with me to the beach that day — she sat guarding her stash of bones left over from the goat barbecue.

'Take your time in the village,' said Minas when I was getting ready to go. 'Don't rush. Take care. Yorgos can help here.'

This new idea of asserting myself appeared to be going well.

All over Greece, the fifteenth of August, the festival of the Holy Virgin, is one of the biggest celebration days of the year. Although I had an inkling of how busy it would be, I didn't know just how special this day was for Olympos. I drove past rows and rows of cars to reach the village entrance in order to throw away our rubbish and was preparing to head half a kilometre back up the road to park when I had a stroke of luck. The couple who had used our 'guest bedroom' at the beach were just about to drive off and gave me their parking spot as well as the money they owed.

I arrived just as everyone was leaving the church in their best clothes, the young women all in traditional, brightly coloured dresses with gold coins hanging around their necks. Carrying a plastic bag of dirty laundry, I felt incredibly awkward, disrespectful even, in my scruffy vest T-shirt and shorts (there was no point in wearing something nice to drive the dirty, smelly Lada and then clean a room). I wished Minas had warned me. From now on, I'd take a dress with me to wear while walking through the village and to meet the guests. Not the skimpy mini-dress I wore at the beach, something more demure.

While waiting for the washing machine to finish another batch of laundry for the rooms, I caught up a bit online. Our internet at the taverna had turned glacially slow because so many people were using it. Sometimes parents would bring their children just so they could use our internet to play games on their tablet. They'd buy a beer and then use up all our data allowance, not realising how limited it was and how desperately we needed it. My laptop had been trying to instal updates and kept turning itself off in frustration.

When I got back to the beach, Minas seemed in a daze, though the kitchen was under control thanks to Speedy George, who now sat calmly on the bench. Fondas cooked slices of swordfish from

Stamatis on the barbecue and shared it with all of us. The campers were driving up to the village for the celebration and dancing and invited me to join them, but I preferred the idea of a rest and some quiet time to myself.

I slept soundly and got up early, taking Lisa down to the beach. She cooled off in the water, then I tied her up and she sat patiently, front paws crossed, while I swam across the bay, wagging her tail when I returned.

Yorgos was already hard at work scouring the kitchen and bathroom – I was happy to have him on the team. He did a great job of keeping the place spotless – though I did worry that he was using half the water tank every morning, and we went through an awful lot of cleaning products. I made breakfast for the new campers, a laid-back group of students who would be staying for a week or so. They painted a piece of driftwood to make a sign for the wall: 'Chillicon Valley'. Towards the end of the morning, Minas took Yorgos down to the beach to distribute free watermelon and raki to people, which was a big hit, and Stamatis also brought in a big catch of fresh fish. We had a busy lunchtime.

Afterwards, I drove up to the village again – this time throwing a sleeveless white linen dress over my vest and shorts to transform my look into something more appropriate as I walked along the alleys and up and down the steps. Flags in bright colours were fluttering around the big church. I took my time cleaning, arranging plant pots in the courtyard, washing dust off the exterior paintwork. I found some pretty cloth in the laundry room and hung it over the fridges in the rooms so they blended better with the traditional décor. I bought some local soap and a little handmade bag for keeping the keys in. When I wasn't in a rush, there was real joy in helping run a small hotel. Our new Dutch visitors were delighted with their room, and it was fun talking with them. Our rooms generally attracted good guests.

Leaving, I stopped for a quick coffee and chat with Georgia, kisses from Maroukla, and a laugh with Marina and Maria, the lovely ladies who sat on either side of the alley where it joined the square; and from Rigopoula I bought a beautiful new cotton blanket. I stopped to see Foula and ask her about the wine her husband made. We needed honey so I bought a kilo from Sophia, and when I popped my head into the restaurant to see Evgenia she gave me a handful of fresh, warm *loukoumades*, the little doughnuts that she made as light as air. They were so delicious I bolted them down at once, so she filled a whole cup and poured honey and sesame seeds liberally over them for me to take. I loved my women friends in the village.

That evening, Minas created a new dessert to tempt people, billed, as always, 'the best you've ever eaten'. This one involved drop pancakes heaped with apple compote and thick cream, drizzled with dark local honey and finished with a dusting of cinnamon. He offered the first one for free, and soon people were ordering another, and one more… Even Vasilis, who often poked suspiciously at the food Minas prepared for him, enjoyed it. There was no debate this time about how he should have made it differently.

The campers who'd been here for weeks sat around in the same group night after night, usually playing guitar and singing. I left Minas with them and pottered around the kitchen. I rather liked putting the fresh produce away, taking stock of what we had, organising the fridge, tidying up.

It was a shame we were always running to keep on top of things. I knew I could help it to work better, and Minas wanted that too.

When things calmed down, I could weigh up the situation. There was so much to love here.

I took some empty cardboard boxes out to the car and suddenly stopped and looked around. The cool breeze felt amazing on my skin. There were so many stars above and an almost-full moon, the hills all around us and no sound but the laughter and music and chatter of our little group.

GOAT

The phone rang and Minas answered it. '*Ela Nick.*' It was his uncle, calling to say they'd had a busy lunchtime up in Olympos. Minas murmured a few things and then said he had to go as he had customers. Then he came to sit back down on the bench, looking out at the empty taverna terrace, and rolled himself a cigarette. Yorgos had done all the cleaning and was also sitting smoking.

'*Ta vasana mou!*' The troubles I have!, Minas groaned. He was looking paler than he had in June, as he so rarely left the taverna except to drive to town. His big shirt hung loosely from his wide shoulders and he looked weary. It was the second half of August, yet business was slow again, and he knew why.

Mustapha was now working for the other taverna. A tall, dark, loose-limbed man from Senegal with a disarming, genuine smile, he wandered around getting to know people on the beach, drumming up business. Minas and he were on friendly terms; Mustapha was a nice guy just making a living. Since we didn't like the idea of hustling people when they were relaxing on the beach, we simply had to do whatever we could too to let people know we were here.

That evening, we considered different initiatives. Minas suggested a flyer that we could get printed in town and hand out to people. It occurred to me that I was usually in the village during the middle of the day when people might be wondering how to spend the rest of the afternoon as they returned to their car, so I could put a sign on the Lada (though the rusty purple tank might not be the greatest advert…). Minas took the idea one step further and suggested I could place flyers on the windscreens of rental cars. It was worth a try.

He borrowed my laptop to design a flyer, advertising not only the food but the fact that we had Wi-Fi and ice cream.

My back was hurting, a trapped nerve in my shoulder that acted up sometimes. I took a sleeping bag and pillow to a cave on the beach. It was a calm night, and although I worried slightly about falling rocks, it was beautiful close to the water's edge, cocooned in a sleeping bag and listening to the hypnotic sound of the waves, the moon very bright above. I'd brought a book and torch, but found the waves mesmerising. I looked up to see a shooting star, then closed my eyes and sleep took over. I woke at sunrise to a pink-tinged sky, the sea still and smooth, then fell asleep again until the sun was warming the beach.

While customers could arrive at any time of day – if they were able to slip through the ever tighter net down on the beach – we always knew we'd be busy in the mornings, serving breakfasts to the campers, most of whom had their habitual coffee time and favourite dish. And because Minas would often drive to town in the morning, I would handle the early rush. I remembered how, years ago when I lived in Montpellier, I worked Sunday mornings in a local bar making breakfasts, and enjoyed it. I also preferred the early shift when I helped at the *kantina* on Tilos.

Since vowing to eat properly, I'd started making heavy-duty toasties with egg, cheese and lashings of bacon for myself, Yorgos and Minas to set us up for the day. Minas was always reminding Yorgos he was welcome to cook whatever he wanted from the kitchen, but he didn't like to, so we tried to make sure we offered him food whenever we were cooking.

'Yorgos, you want a *tostaki*?' I said, handing him his usual on a plate.

Normally he was grateful but today he just said, 'Later,' which seemed oddly rude. Maybe he was in a bad mood because as soon as he'd cleaned the orange juice machine, someone ordered another one and he'd have to do it all over again. But he was usually happy enough.

'I won't be here to cook one later,' I reminded him. 'I have to go to the village.'

It was a little ridiculous to be driving half an hour to the village practically every day. With so much going on, and so much work required for a changeover, single-night bookings made no sense at all, but Minas had accepted most of these reservations months ago, without specifying check-in and check-out times. As soon as he got back from town to deal with lunch, I drove off in the Lada, and then had to spend time putting flyers on car windscreens before hurrying to the rooms. I stopped at his uncle's taverna to pick up the keys.

'Evgenia,' said Nick. 'The people went into their room, but they said it was very dirty. They don't like it.'

'Yes, it's very dirty!' his waitress chimed in.

'That's because I haven't had time to clean it yet,' I explained, sighing.

I found the guests and let them know their room would be ready in about an hour. That wasn't a problem at all, they said – they had arrived early, completely understood and just needed a place to leave their bags.

The key for the upstairs room was missing, and I had to break in again by climbing over the balcony, getting funny looks from passers-by. I found the key inside – with a five-euro tip, which made me forgive the people instantly. But when I saw myself in the mirror while bundling up the sheets, I got a shock. My face looked tired and I was thin, my ribs showing. I couldn't do this much longer.

The laundry, ironing and cleaning left me exhausted, but the guests were delighted with their room, which made it feel worthwhile. Minas called to say he'd had a busy hour, thanks to the flyers. He also said I should go to the post office and try to find a bill for our internet service, because the internet wasn't working and perhaps we'd been cut off, which would be a little embarrassing since our flyers advertised free Wi-Fi. He added, 'There are fifty people still on the beach, so get down here soon.'

I bought more chocolate to eat in the car.

I passed most of the fifty people driving up the track as I drove down, but there were still a couple of tables to deal with. Then it was just us and the campers. Yorgos, usually so cheerful, was in a foul mood, tired and grumpy, so I insisted he take the rest of the evening off. Lisa was happily wandering around, looking for treats and strokes. She was the only member of the team not exhausted and ready to quit. When Minas announced he was making spaghetti for dinner for the campers, I jumped in and ordered myself a portion.

'I gotta take a nap first,' he said, lying on a bench and covering himself with a sleeping bag. 'Can you finish the sauce, and wake me in exactly forty-five minutes?'

Ah, the famous forty-five minutes... After forty-five minutes, he wouldn't wake up, so I made and served everyone spaghetti myself.

❖ ❖ ❖ ❖

A skinny grey-white goat had been wandering around the valley for weeks looking very feeble, as if it was going to die. I think we all knew how it felt.

Every morning, dozens of goats would stream down from the hills into the valley, marauding – on a mission to help themselves to the olive trees. We encouraged Lisa to bark to shoo them away. Minas's aunt Sophia and his cousin Evgenia usually rounded up their animals and kept them fed and watered at their farm in Argoni on the other side of the ridge from Vasilis.

But some goats refused to go, and this one, now that it had finished off our seedlings, was struggling to fend for itself in the wild. It had grown so weak that we were able to grab it by the horns one morning, and Minas tied it to a tree so we could give it water and keep it safe. Then Sophia or Evgenia could take it away when they got a break from their restaurant in the village later in the day. Lisa found the whole thing intriguing. We kept her on the lead for her walk and then tied her in the shade of the fig tree, her favourite spot, from where she could greet all the customers as they arrived.

A group of three Greek friends who were staying in our village rooms for a few days showed up at the beach around noon. The trio – a rather glamorous woman, a young man and an older man with a paunch and a long grey ponytail – ordered a carafe of raki and played backgammon and guitar. They asked me about the wedding due to take place at the church on the cliffs that day. Often, traditional island weddings are open to everyone; the Athenians had heard about it and were hoping to go along.

'We don't really know anything about it,' I said, having checked with Minas. A group of local men had arrived from the village that morning for coffee and told us they were doing the preparations, the first we'd heard about a wedding. 'But we expect it will start sometime in the afternoon.'

Apart from our days, most things started late.

The trio continued drinking and ordered a couple of plates of food between them. Slowly a strange atmosphere developed, spearheaded by Mr Ponytail.

'Why do you keep your dog tied up?' he asked in a belligerent tone.

'She's not always tied up,' I explained, 'but we don't want her in the restaurant in the middle of the day, or running away and chasing goats. She's part hunting dog, and we have to keep her and the goats safe.'

'I'm an artist,' he said. 'I believe in freedom.'

Although the trio had initially been friendly, I was getting an odd feeling from them, a sense that they didn't much like us. I looked up towards the church, hoping to see something happening so they'd be on their way. The woman said something under her breath that made Ponytail laugh.

We ignored it – they were just drunk. We had good music playing, and were busy making lunches for two large families, one Greek and one Austrian, who were camping on the beach. Then suddenly I heard barking. It turned out Ponytail had decided to set Lisa free. Of course, she had immediately raced to the goat that was tied to a tree, the goat we were trying to keep safe.

We finished off the food orders and excused ourselves to deal with the problem. We needed to catch Lisa but that was easier said than done. She could be extremely strong-willed and clever. There was no way she'd let me or Minas catch her when she had a goat in her sights – she nimbly slipped through our fingers each time we came close. We stood near the worried goat to block her from getting to it, but she skipped back and forth and circled it, unable to leave it alone or stop barking. Of course, the barking was bound to alert everyone to the situation.

Thankfully, we had something she couldn't resist in the fridge, and Minas went to get it. She knew it meant losing her freedom and the excitement of this game, but better a fresh, juicy lamb chop in the mouth than a hairy, skinny old goat tied to a tree. We grabbed her by the collar and brought her back to the taverna, apologising to the customers for the minor disruption. We asked Ponytail to leave our dog alone and took the trio their bill, suggesting it might be time for them to be on their way.

'Oh yes, we'll just go to the *wedding*,' said the woman sarcastically. 'This so-called wedding you've been talking about all day just so you can take our money.'

Thankfully, they disappeared. And soon Sophia showed up to take her goat. Much, much later, after midnight, when just a few of us were sitting around sipping drinks and talking, I heard music coming from the church – the wedding was starting.

The next day as I drove up to the village, I worried about what the strange trio might have done to their room. They didn't seem like our usual lovely guests. Could they have damaged things and left without paying? Should we ask them to leave? I parked and put flyers on car windshields as I walked in.

I shakily knocked on their door, prepared for a confrontation. The door opened, and it was dark inside. They were sleeping off the booze, and sheepishly apologised.

Heartily relieved, I said it was no problem, and got on with cleaning the other room. While ascending the steps, I overheard some visitors on the doorstep talking to each other about the views, so I invited them in and showed them the traditional bed and the balcony, and told them we hoped to see them next year.

Leaving, I hunted through the box of post outside the souvlaki shop and found Minas's electricity bill – as well as a letter for me from Germany. I opened it up and found a card from a woman who had come here in June. She'd sent us the red peppercorns she'd told us about. It felt so long ago. How nice of her.

'When are you going back to England?' asked Rigopoula's husband as I passed them a little further down the alley.

'Not for a long time!' I said. 'Why – you want me to bring you the Marbles?'

Changing over rooms wasn't the most glamorous work, but it had its rewards. And it was still a spectacular drive. I got back to the beach in time to swim before the sun disappeared, noticing Minas had some customers.

'Remember the women I gave the fish soup to months ago?' he asked.

Of course I remembered. He had gone to lots of trouble to make fish soup but no-one was ordering it. He was always convinced that if people tried the food, they would have confidence to order something, and he was sometimes right. So when two Greek women had stopped in that day just to use the bathroom and buy a cold drink on their way home, he had insisted on giving them shots of raki and bowls of fish soup. They weren't hungry, they insisted, as they had just had lunch elsewhere. One of them had made a polite effort, but the other barely touched her soup, even though she said it was very good. It had caused him no end of grief at the time. But it turned out they recommended the place to their friends, who had come this evening and were eating fresh fish. It really was a long-term game.

Since the barbecue was hot and the work was done, I experimented with cooking *skaros* for myself the way Minas did. We had a serrated scraper for removing the scales. I used scissors to cut its belly up to the neck, pulled the guts out until it was clean inside; rubbed a little olive oil on it, added a couple of slices of lemon and a sprig of rosemary, wrapped it in foil and put it on the grill. It turned out good, but not perfect. I'd missed a few scales around the edges and there was a slight bitterness where I must have missed something cleaning it. I needed more practice and would try it directly on the grill next time to crisp the skin.

It was late August, four months since I'd first arrived; an intense four months. Now, I could scarcely believe it but the evenings were finally getting quieter; the big group with their guitars was gradually breaking up as people went home or moved on to another island. With Yorgos helping us, in the evenings and mornings I often had time again to run with Lisa up the hill to the church. At 10pm, there was no-one around, just Minas and our friend Dinos snoring in the corner, and the same old soundtrack playing, and I could take a walk on the beach in the dark and quiet.

It was a warm, calm night. I liked it, but I knew we could do with a few more busy days, a week or two more of business. Minas felt bad because the takings for the year would mostly go towards paying his debts. He'd invested so much and he desperately wanted to do better. The moon cast a pathway of cherry-tinged light on the water. I watched it turn to pale lemon yellow and rise towards the church on the cliffs. Then Lisa started barking. Perhaps a new group of campers had arrived on the late boat. Or maybe the goat was back.

The next morning, I noticed the radio was on, playing different songs from those on the playlist we'd been listening to all summer. Even Minas was sick of the music he'd chosen at the start of the season and that we had listened to several times a day, every day.

New campers had indeed arrived. In the village, a few weeks earlier, I'd been carrying half a barrel of olive oil from Minas's house to the Lada when a young guy had kindly offered to help. He'd asked where I was staying, out of curiosity, and I told him about the beach. He had obviously decided to come back with a couple of women friends. The summer wasn't quite over, not yet.

Minas was still researching the rules about planting umbrellas in the beach in a conservation zone. The neighbour was still escorting customers to her taverna, and Minas took photos as a warning that he could report it if this continued. Later that day, when he was driving past their taverna, her husband came over, reached through the window and punched him. I was horrified, but Minas appeared delighted, grinning, showing off his bruised eye.

'I want him to do it again, so I can get a restraining order and he'll have to leave!'

Stamatis arrived with his usual bright greeting to match his bright pink T-shirt and carrying a cool box full of fish, some of their tails still flapping. He asked me for his customary weak iced coffee and had a power nap lying on the bench, then sat barefoot on the terrace floor, his legs out in front of him, patiently baiting what seemed like hundreds of small hooks with prawns for longline fishing. Minas had installed a separate fridge out the back just for fishing bait and ice.

Sergei sat beside him on a chair wearing skimpy swimming trunks and drinking raki, occasionally pointing at his empty glass for a refill. Stamatis perhaps should have had a rule about not drinking while working – but the fishermen worked from before dawn until after dark most days, and lunchtime was their rest time. Sergei finally strutted off down the now dry rocky path between the olive trees in his Speedos, with the empty cool box on his shoulder.

At lunchtime, I helped out by making a couple of salads and fried potatoes, squeezed some fresh orange juice. I laughed with the customers, using a few words of Italian I'd picked up over the summer.

Stamatis bringing in the fresh catch had worked magic, and we were soon mildly busy with the business we needed. By mid-afternoon, Minas had drunk a gazillion beers and was singing rock songs, being filmed on smartphones. But it was amazing how he could sober up when needed to cook. An Italian couple, Anna and Giuseppe, chose a large grouper – '*Cernia!*' – from the fresh catch and reserved it for a special romantic dinner.

In early evening, Giuseppe left Anna to enjoy the last of the sun on the beach while he came up and ordered a half-litre of cold white wine and chatted with Minas, watching him grill the fish to perfection over the charcoal. His wife had a shower, then the couple enjoyed the fading light in the quiet valley and said what a special place it was as we served mezes and fish. Afterwards, I cut them some watermelon, and Minas brought out the raki and sat with them. People loved learning about the food and the place from him, and he made them laugh with his stories. It was an essential part of the experience, turning customers into friends and completing the happy memories that often made them return year after year.

All was well, except that Yorgos was sitting on the bench outside the kitchen, fuming because he hadn't eaten yet and Minas had said he would make him dinner. To Yorgos, it seemed that Minas was just sitting around drinking. I explained that he was busy and that Yorgos should go and help himself to whatever he wanted from the kitchen. There was plenty of food. If he had a complaint, now was not the time.

Yorgos had been behaving oddly the last few days. Maybe it was the tension of the umbrella wars. That afternoon, the neighbour had threatened Minas with violence again, sending a message via Sergei.

'Are we ever going to eat?' Yorgos suddenly shouted across to Minas.

Minas shouted back at him, and they argued back and forth for a couple of minutes. Thankfully it was all in Greek so the guests didn't understand, though they probably caught the tone. Finally, exasperated, Minas said, 'You know how to fry a pork chop. And if you're not happy, you can pack your bag, take your money and leave.' He asked me to count out what we owed Yorgos and hand it to him so he had the choice.

And Yorgos went to the little house and packed his bag. Maybe he'd been thinking about it for a while. He sat and drank a glass of raki, and as soon as there was a truck going up to the road, he left. As Minas sang his favourite song for our guests, I thought at least now I'd have somewhere to go when I needed to escape the Hard Rock Café.

The couple decided it was time to leave, but Anna was scared to go up the dirt track after her husband had been drinking, in the dark with the wind blowing, and on the back of a scooter. We had no idea they'd come on a scooter, which wasn't the best vehicle for these tracks. Minas insisted on driving her the few kilometres to the main road in the Lada, which thankfully had been cleaned the day before and didn't smell too badly of rubbish, while Giuseppe followed on the scooter. And so they set off.

Lisa was loose – we often let her free for a bit in the evenings when the goats had been rounded up – and unfortunately decided to chase the convoy, barking excitedly all the way. There was nothing I could do about it – she'd come back when Minas did. Given that our kitchen help had just quit, I began to clean up and organise the fridges. After ten minutes or so, the phone rang; it was one of the hotel guests wanting to know about boat trips. I tried to find the phone numbers of the boat captains on the Skype account on my laptop, but my battery was giving up the ghost. Then I heard a fuss outside.

It turned out that Minas had driven Anna up the dirt road at speed, chatting along the way, while she complained about her husband only renting a scooter instead of a car. They had reached the top of the road and sat waiting for Giuseppe. As they waited and waited, the small talk had dried up, each increasingly concerned that Giuseppe had veered off the road, perhaps blown by the wind, or taken a wrong turn and fallen down the steep drop into the valley. He didn't answer his phone. They started to drive back down and peered in the dark for signs of the scooter.

Meanwhile, Giuseppe, halfway up the dirt road, had worried about Lisa chasing him, thinking it was dangerous for her, and decided to turn back. He arrived at the taverna thinking he was a hero for bringing back our dog safely.

A very shaken Anna quickly got over her concern about potentially being widowed and laid into him in a way that all of us could understand whether we spoke Italian or not. Lisa looked very pleased with herself. We tied her up, and they set off again.

When I went to check on the little house, I found the litre-and-a-half bottle of raki that Yorgos had insisted on buying for himself a few days ago, almost empty. Perhaps that explained his odd behaviour. But then maybe we were all behaving oddly.

DANCING

At the end of August, there was a festival in the far north of the island with traditional music and dancing. Minas insisted we should go, hear the music, dance a little, sleep at his family's cottage in Avlona and cut some grapes and figs in the morning.

It was the kind of thing I'd usually love, but fatigue took the appeal out of driving all that way; my body ached constantly, I didn't have appropriate clothes, and everything started so late. What's more, I was afraid to leave Lisa alone with the neighbours around and acting aggressively. Minas, however, said he wanted to show me more of island life and introduce me to some people. Our camper friend Yiannis would come too; though he now lived in Athens, he was originally from this island and, after the others left, was staying on for a while in the driftwood beach shelter that his girlfriend Theresa had built. It gradually came to feel as though it would be a rather special outing. I ate a big bowl of yoghurt and honey for energy as we lounged on the benches for a while, resting, to be ready to go out later. Then Minas announced he didn't want to go after all, and was asleep within minutes. He really could be exasperating.

For the next couple of days, business was quiet. Yorgos, we'd heard, was in the village and, now he'd sobered up, would come back if we needed him; but we didn't need anyone now that the busiest days of the season were over. I left the taverna to Minas while I did my own work in the *spitaki*. In my business, people were returning to their offices after the summer, and I should be back at my desk, wherever that desk was, from time to time. I felt ready for a change, anyway. The little house was still piled high with boxes, but a mattress on a wooden platform made a comfortable couch for working, with a gorgeous view of olive trees, the church on the cliffs, and a sliver of blue sea. It was peaceful and perfect. I suddenly remembered this was exactly what I'd hoped for when Minas first told me about spending the summer here: a simple little house in the middle of nowhere near the sea.

'Just shout if you need me,' I had said.

'Don't worry, I'm sure I can handle it,' Minas had replied sardonically, given the way things were looking.

But in the early afternoon, Sergei came over to say Minas needed me. I closed my laptop and went over to find a buzzing taverna, filled with mostly returning customers. Once again, it seemed, the season wasn't over after all: it had merely changed.

At one of the tables was a Czech couple in their thirties who had been coming to this beach for years. They had recently got married, and had invited a couple of dozen friends to an informal celebration at the church on the cliffs that coming Saturday. They would spend the afternoon at the beach and come to the taverna for food and drinks. They would then drive back to where they were staying, in an area in the south of the island where people came for windsurfing, for a big party that same night. We would be welcome to join them.

After a busy afternoon, Minas settled down for a snooze when the last vehicles left the beach. With no campers around now, it was unlikely anyone else would turn up. I walked to the beach, guessing that when I got back he'd be so fast asleep I could turn the music off, make a cup of tea and sit at my computer. I wished it could always be about days like this: preparing good food and creating a great atmosphere, making people happy; enough business to tick over nicely, with time to myself and to enjoy the surroundings. How beautiful it could be here in the winter, I thought, looking around at the hills, rugged and elemental and unspoiled. I sat in the taverna until close to midnight, relishing the peace, the solitude, the sound of the wind in the trees.

Minas bought a lobster from Stamatis – a *karavitha*, technically a large crayfish – and we offered it to customers for a couple of days but had no takers. I felt so sorry for the poor thing, kept alive in the kitchen awaiting its fate. Minas gave in and cooked the lobster one night when Mustapha came over with a couple of friends who had been working in tavernas all summer and had their first night off in months. There was nobody around so we turned the lights down and moved the tables aside. The lads, who were from Senegal and Pakistan, found some great music online and we all danced for an hour or so, leaving the worries of the season behind. When Minas invited Mustapha to come with us to the Czech party on Saturday night, he said he probably couldn't if we were staying over because on Sunday morning they were taking down the umbrellas and the neighbours would soon be leaving.

In a celebratory mood ourselves, we had fun coming up with ideas for the wedding party, and the next day Minas drove to town to buy supplies, balloons and the fixings for baking and icing a cake. There were unusual sounds coming from around the other taverna – could they be the sounds of packing up? I didn't dare think about it. How relaxing it would be if we had the valley to ourselves again.

On Saturday morning, it was very windy as we prepared to decorate the taverna. Neither of us had blown up a balloon in years, and we fell about laughing as we tried to get the hang of it. We started to tie the pink balloons to the wooden columns that held up the pergola, but almost as fast as we tied them, the wind wrenched them off and down the field, or knocked them about until they burst. We tried attaching them to stones instead, in the shelter of the windows, with more success. We also tied big white bows on the entrance, and all the pink and white looked very striking against the wooden taverna in the middle of the summer-parched golden fields and olive groves. Minas painted a beach stone as a gift and put the final touches on the pink and white wedding cake. We arranged the blue tables in a line and glasses in two long rows, and prepared an ice bucket – actually one of those handy five-kilo yoghurt tubs, covered in tin foil – for a few bottles of rosé bubbly.

Thankfully about half the balloons were still in place when the guests started to arrive and crack open a few beers. The bride chilled out in a bikini. Eventually, we all drove or walked up to the clifftop church, brilliant white against the sapphire blue of the sea. One of the boys, wearing just shorts, sunglasses and a bow tie, pulled on the rope to ring the bell. The bride made her appearance barefoot, blushing and tanned in a strapless white dress with wildflowers in her hair. We all gathered around, and one of the restaurant owners from the village, officiating as an ersatz priest, called for quiet.

'Do you, crazy Czech tourist, take this man to be your husband?' She said she did.

'Are you *sure*?'

There was plenty of banter and laughter, then we all went down to the pink-themed taverna and celebrated. The group spent the rest of the afternoon at the beach. We were happy to have been part of their special celebration – and maybe it could be the start of more such events. We were more or less alone when Stamatis arrived, coincidentally wearing a pink T-shirt – with news of an incident that had occurred while we were up at the church.

That morning, a couple had arrived at the beach in their jeep and been approached to rent umbrellas. They declined, walked away to the end of the beach and instead made use of Theresa and Yiannis's empty driftwood shelter for a couple of hours. When the visitors left, the neighbour stomped darkly across the beach and tore down the shelter. She threatened Stamatis too, saying that both he and Minas would be gone next year. I'd never seen Stamatis angry before now. Yiannis was going to be even angrier when he returned the next day from visiting his father.

We had a few tables in late afternoon and then cleared up at an easy pace. I assumed Minas would soon change his mind about driving all the way to the south of the island to party with the Czechs; or would insist on going and then fall asleep. I wasn't at all in the mood for driving for an hour and a half in the dark with no radio in the car, hungry and tired.

But Minas seemed determined we should go. He said we'd eat when we got there – the party was being held at a taverna, and there were nice rooms where we could get a good night's sleep. It was starting to sound more appealing, except that now I was really scared of leaving Lisa overnight, with the neighbour acting so strangely and destructively. Minas insisted it would be worse for Lisa to be stuck in the car all night, and the neighbours were no longer here in the evenings. I had a quiet word with Mustapha, and he said he'd look after her.

As we drove up the track and along the winding mountain road, I realised just how dim our headlights were. The west coast road went through a mostly wild area. With little to see along the way in the dark of night, the drive passed slowly and all I could think about was ordering a big jug of wine and dinner, and going to sleep in a comfortable bed. An hour and a half later, we descended to the south coast and skirted the little island airport, following a sign for our destination; the road turned narrow and dark, with fields on either side.

Then, suddenly, there were lights and heaps of cars. We parked and heard thumping dance music playing very loud. It didn't look anything like a taverna... It looked like an open-air nightclub with people leaping about, silhouetted against the bright lights. When we got to the top of the steps, where a wooden deck was serving as bar and dance floor, we spotted a table and the sad, bedraggled remains of a buffet. Minas set off to find someone we knew and ask about the rooms. I found a windsurfer dude behind the bar and shouted to him over the noise, pointing at a familiar-looking wine box in the fridge. As he poured a little into a cup, I wanted to say, 'Leave the box.'

Minas returned with the news that all the rooms were fully booked for the wedding.

I rolled my eyes. 'So, no food and no room...'

'OK, we can drive straight back home if you want.'

He was right, those really were the two options – or driving somewhere else. But there was no way I was getting back in the car. I knocked back my glass of wine and Minas got us some more. The music started to sound pretty good. There was only one thing for it... A few glasses of wine and we joined the throng leaping about, laughing and doing silly, crazy dancing. At one point, I must have done something a little athletic and pulled a muscle in my hip, but I didn't want to admit even to myself that I was that old, so I danced through the pain... For hours we did dancing therapy, letting loose to all sorts of music under the stars.

I woke up at dawn on a bean bag under a blanket, surrounded by kite-surfing equipment and lots of other people crashed out on bean bags, and limped my way across to the sandy, windswept beach. The nightclub had transformed itself back into a café, and we ordered frappe and toast. Then we drove back up to the north of the island in the sunshine on a quiet Sunday morning in early September, Minas comparing the quality and price of their breakfast offerings to ours, me anxiously hoping Lisa was OK, and both of us speculating on whether there would still be umbrellas on the beach.

Arriving back still felt wonderful as the track wound around the pine-covered hillsides to the olive-filled valley and blue bay. It was good to be home, and Lisa was barking and doing a little dance from side to side, leaping up, her ears sticking out from her head. It looked as though she'd been sleeping and only woken up when the Lada turned the last steep twist in the road. I'd thank Mustapha later for looking after her.

We gave her some attention, then showered and changed and made proper cheese and bacon toasties. For now, the umbrellas were still on the beach with Mustapha manning them, but the neighbours' taverna seemed to be closed and there was no sign of them, which meant we had more business than usual. Stamatis arrived in his boat with a fresh catch, and from noon until dusk I was limping around with my dancing injury serving lovely customers from Italy, Austria, Belgium and Portugal, all eating fish and salads and having a great time. Whenever I asked, 'Is everything OK?' people looked dreamy and said, 'Perfect…' I was already liking September.

Our camper friend Yiannis arrived back in the evening and was outraged that the beach shelter had been torn down – it was just as well for her sake that the perpetrator wasn't around. Rumour had it that she could have already left the island for the season. Perhaps she had her own reasons for acting the way she did, but cheekily I imagined an evil cackle as she vowed to rule the world then disappeared in a puff of smoke.

I finally had the dinner I'd hoped for the night before, a heaped Greek salad and lamb chops – there really was no taverna like home. When Lisa and Minas were both snoozing side by side, I had peace and quiet to read. With no-one about in the evenings, we could fall asleep on the cushioned benches after dusk.

After a night so quiet I'd been able to hear the sea lapping at the rocks from the taverna, the morning was completely still, the sea glassy calm. Minas headed into the kitchen, saying he'd heard something else in the night, maybe a cat had got inside. But no. Half the ceiling had fallen down, taking the light fixtures with it.

Without a proper window in the back of the kitchen it was dark, but clear enough to see chunks of plaster all over the kitchen floor. Minas insisted that all the ceiling that was going to fall had fallen, but I wasn't convinced. How could he know that? I was afraid to go in, especially after he told me that he knew the roof should have been replaced and the ceiling was questionable. It could easily have fallen around our heads at any time.

Shaken by the thought that we'd been working in those conditions, I remembered the hazardous episode of the exploding hot water tank. And driving the Lada up and down that road while the seat gradually shifted so far forward I could hardly get out. Having to leave Lisa here on her own. Putting myself and Lisa in potential danger while I took care of business. Things never quite got properly fixed, it seemed. Feeling upset, I recounted the litany of things that had wrong: broken water filter, broken ice machine, empty water tank… The washing machine still didn't make clothes clean, just wet, and had to be turned on using a screwdriver. 'What's next?'

'I don't know what you're saying,' Minas replied, gritting his teeth.

I let him get on with clearing up the mess and drove up to the village to spend the day changing over the rooms, taking my time, catching up on laundry, pressing sheets and scalding my fingers on the steam. Just the day before, things had felt so peaceful and good, but now, once again, my mind was besieged by doubts and worries about life here. I didn't mind hard work, but hard work in hazardous conditions was something else. How much did he care about my welfare if he was happy to let me work in a kitchen with a ceiling that could fall on my head? I still appreciated the way he wanted me to share everything, I loved the idea of being part of it all, but if it was always falling to pieces, did I really want that? And with someone who thought that was normal?

I drove back down to the beach but Minas and I didn't talk much. As if echoing my feelings, the weather turned very cold that night and for some reason Lisa woke me, whining. Unable to get back to sleep for a while, I looked at the ferry schedules and saw there was a ferry leaving the next day. Minas wouldn't have too much difficulty handling things alone now if I went, and he could hire Yorgos back. I'd thought about walking out before, and yet I'd stayed, I'd always stayed – not just from a sense of integrity about keeping my word, but because somehow once the mood was better, we just got back to work. Because I loved it here and it would be a heartbreaking wrench to tear myself away. The only way to leave would be to leave quickly...

Eventually I got back to sleep. When I woke, feeling rested, listening to the birds as the sun began to warm the valley again, I put things in perspective. I do sometimes overreact to perceived injustices. I had several times slept in a beach cave that was at least as risky as the kitchen. If this were an easy place to live, we wouldn't have it to ourselves. It was amazing we could live here at all, and that was thanks to Minas and his ability to fix things. This was an adventure and an experiment in a different way of living, so why would I expect it to be smooth and untroubled?

I'd been concerned about other things, too, like my own work, which brought its own share of headaches. I'd been taking on too much, unnecessarily as my bank account was healthy after several months with little in the way of expenses. The weather was perfect and it would be a shame to leave now that things were becoming calmer. I cancelled some work travel plans for October, which felt the right thing to do for myself. I decided to rest and enjoy September here, then go home to my house for a while. I'd made new friends all summer, but I also missed my old ones. After that, I wasn't exactly sure.

When I saw the ferry pass far out to sea at lunchtime, the mood was happy again and I felt I'd made the right decision by staying. I hadn't told Minas about my impulse to flee the previous night, though he was far from stupid and may have guessed what I was thinking. He had knocked the remaining plaster from the ceiling for now and rigged up a new ceiling light. Together we looked after a few lunchtime tables, then he suggested I go and have some time to myself. I went to the beach and fell asleep on the sun-warmed pebbles to the sound of the waves and woke feeling even better.

When I returned to the taverna, Minas and his friend Pavlos were chatting quietly and drinking beer, talking over some building ideas. It did him good to unwind, too, and have someone else to talk to. A few people came and went for drinks and ice creams. We hoped to sell through lots of stock over the coming weeks and shut down one of the fridges and the ice-cream freezer (which gave Minas an excuse to eat chocolate Magnums for dinner). I cut some fruit for myself then took a book back down to the beach and stayed there from late afternoon to early evening, until the sea was a deep denim blue and the sky its usual blissful pink. The sunbeds were collected off the beach that same afternoon and disappeared, though the umbrellas themselves remained. The ceiling had indeed stopped falling, at least for now.

Every day the weather was calm, the sea warm, the beach still too hot to stand on barefoot in the midday sun. There weren't many customers, not enough for two tavernas, but just enough for us to stay open. We had time to get to know them, a mix of interesting people from all over Europe. Many told us how scary it was driving down here, and then had a cold beer and relaxed; we showed them the fresh fish of the day and they stayed for lunch. Some Austrians left behind a pair of spectacles one day, so they returned for lunch later in the week – and then the same man forgot his hat. In the village, our guests continued to lock their keys in their rooms, and I never found a spare set; as soon as the bookings stopped, we would need to take the keys to town and get some extra sets cut, and labelled, and stored properly.

One evening, as I was lying at the far end of the beach after a swim, a truck arrived and a group of guys removed the umbrellas. It was an exciting moment, though I was dismayed to see them leave two rows of ugly metal stumps sticking out of the sand, plugged with old bits of clothing, where the umbrella bases were buried in this beautiful, natural beach – all for two months' worth of money-making. I sympathised with Minas's efforts to get the local authorities to clamp down. That fight would have to go on, somehow. But for now, it seemed, things might be a little calmer.

It was glorious to wake up to the sounds not of howling wind but of birds and the sea lapping and slapping against the rocks.

I swam across the bay, the water so clear and still I could see my shadow on the seabed. Then I lay on a sarong on the warm pebbles, glad to be still here, at this beach. I managed to get Minas to help clean the kitchen before driving to town, reminding him that I had my own work to do.

Yorgos, our old pal Speedy George, had spent a couple of weeks doing building work with Pavlos and came down to the valley to help water Rigopoula's olive trees. When Pavlos came to visit us, Minas welcomed Yorgos too, cooking him a big meal and telling him we'd be happy for him to return next year for the whole summer if he wanted. When they left, he put on the radio and fell asleep early, next to a table covered in beer bottle caps, flecks of tobacco and an ice-cream wrapper. I went for my late afternoon swim, the beach to myself again, then took Lisa for a walk up the valley. It was getting dark earlier, and I returned to the black silhouettes of olive trees against the warm glow of the taverna, with a sharp, bright sliver of crescent moon and stars emerging in the dark blue sky above.

❖ ❖ ❖ ❖

It should have been plain sailing from now on; but then a couple of things happened. It started when Stamatis's familiar white fishing boat was missing from the bay for a couple of days. At last he called to explain why.

Usually when we'd selected the fish we wanted for the day, Stamatis would drive in his van to the villages to sell the rest of the catch – what he made from us wasn't nearly enough for him to run the boat. Sergei would be helping him and probably drinking raki at every stop. One day while Stamatis was busy, he'd left Sergei to look after the van, and Sergei had somehow managed to drive it into the side of a mountain; then left it there with the engine running, so the engine burned out. He even refused to help rescue the van and left the fish inside to go bad.

Without the van, Stamatis couldn't work. It was spectacularly bad timing, as he had to make his money while the restaurants remained open for the season. The sight of Sergei sitting in his swimming trunks pointing at his raki glass would be a mere memory. Knowing our fresh fish supply would be more erratic for the rest of September, Minas seemed tense.

Meanwhile, he was trying to convince me that we should buy a secondhand espresso machine from someone he knew. When Italians wanted coffee after lunch, they were often hugely relieved that we offered espresso but we had just one percolator, which had made things tricky during the busy live-music days of summer when people ordered multiple espressos simultaneously. Still, espresso machines were expensive.

He said we could have this one for free and would only have to pay if he could fix it. This sounded an odd arrangement, and I suspected it was the kind of thing that led to unexpected debts. I also had visions of yet another piece of broken machinery lying around. Even the lights that had fallen off the kitchen ceiling had been kept as he wanted to 'strip them for parts'. I suggested he might want to start fixing some things during the quiet times, rather than sitting around getting anxious.

'Do you know where the glue is?' he asked.

I told him, and he took it and later told me the ice machine was working.

'Hallelujah! So what happened?' I asked.

'I fixed it,' he replied tersely. 'It was broken. And I fixed it. With glue.'

'But I meant, how did you do it?' I was pleased and curious.

He recounted every technical detail, proving he knew how to fix broken machinery in a way I didn't understand. I asked him why he was acting like this, and he replied that I found fault with everything, that he had a hundred things on his mind…

'What can I do to help?' I asked.

'Nothing. I usually have more business when you're not here, so take a day off.'

I wished he'd said it in a nicer way.

The frosty atmosphere made me miserable, and because I needed the internet for my work, I ended up sitting in a full, busy restaurant, having to ignore the customers, which just felt stupid.

In the evening I tried talking to Minas, but it seemed to make things worse. He turned the music up loud, so I took a sleeping bag and a book and some wine down to the beach, to a clearing in the trees made by the campers. A few clouds had been gathering and I watched them crossing the moon, darkening the valley. For years I'd thought about sleeping on the beach from time to time, and now I was doing it often. Whatever happened from now on, I'd done what I hoped for, spent a whole summer by the sea. I woke at dawn and watched the blood-orange, peachy clouds as the sun rose.

After sitting at my laptop doing my own work all morning, around noon I went into the kitchen to make fresh bread. I was kneading dough when customers started arriving, and Minas and I slipped into serving lunch together as if nothing had happened.

As a table of four finished their meal, he asked me, 'Did you tell them it's my birthday?'

I went to get the raki bottle and four shot glasses.

'You must drink also with us!' the people said to us. So we did.

It was convivial, and when everyone had left and the sun had gone from the beach, Minas switched off the music, and I cooked myself some food and continued with work. He sat browsing news online, the mood companionable. His back had been hurting, and the end of season must be hard. He didn't seem to want to talk about it, but I believed we both understood the situation; maybe he also had other things on his mind that he couldn't discuss with me. He wouldn't be seeing much of his friends until next summer, and wouldn't be making music. Probably at the end of every season, there was a time of wondering who would be moving on and to where. In the early hours of the morning, I woke up to see him still sitting on the terrace with the lights on, listening to the radio, smoking.

I tried not to think about what would come next but take it day by day. If things got better, I'd love to spend longer here with Minas, without other people around, and consider the future. If things got worse, I could now walk away knowing I'd tried. There was no point in worrying – everything would work out as it should. After September, I'd see how I felt and decide what to do for the winter. Perhaps he was thinking about that, and whether he'd be spending the winter here.

In all the months I'd lived at the taverna, I still hadn't walked the half-hour to Nati, the next beach over the headland to the north. When I woke early to mauve clouds over the sea, the torn bottom of the tent flapping in a breeze, I decided to go. Even before the sun filled the valley I threw on a bikini top, jean shorts and trainers, grabbed Lisa and headed off, following the track twisting down into a wild valley, where we startled some partridges and a lot of goats, to a beach of sand and flat pebbles gently shelving into sea as clear as glass.

Lisa and I took turns going for a swim. The sky was blue but with a bank of dark grey cloud.

I've no idea why, but that evening the tension between Minas and me returned. Whatever was said – the confrontation got heated and I don't remember – an exchange exploded into an emotionally fraught argument. After a while I stopped responding, telling myself that the anger wasn't about me but about him letting off steam, but I felt sick and shaky. I didn't want this, I thought; it was wrong. I closed my eyes, knowing that this time when he fell asleep I would quietly pack up my things, take the money owed to me, and leave in the night. I could walk all the way to the port, and catch the next boat.

As if reading my thoughts, he said that if I wanted to leave I should tell him what he owed me so I wouldn't feel cheated and leave unhappy.

There were a few minutes of quiet, and then he asked me what I wanted for dinner.

How could he think I wanted him to make me dinner? It was absurd.

Perhaps what had just happened was his idea of talking. And, knowing he liked to cook for people he loved, perhaps this was a sort of apology, or at least an attempt at reconciliation.

I walked to the beach. The sea was silver and the valley was flooded with the strange otherworldly brightness of moonlight.

It was as if a huge storm had passed.

END OF THE SEASON

It took a while and a conversation, but an atmosphere of trust returned. The mood between Minas and me was good again, and I felt hugely relieved. I hoped that was the last of the anxiety coming out, and we could get along from now on. We agreed to go to the village together for the first time since the start of summer to see his friends who were visiting from Malta and staying at our rooms. He'd drunk a fair bit with customers that afternoon, so I insisted on taking the wheel.

The rusty purple Lada had been a reliable member of the team, never giving us a problem even as she plied the long road across the island filled with crates of beer, or slalomed down the bumpy track as fast as Minas could drive doing the ice cream run. Sure, something needed to be unplugged if she was going to be left alone a few days or the battery would be drained, and sure, the lack of a seriously effective handbrake worried me a lot when I had the time to think about it. The driver window could only be wound up using a wrench, and the back door of course was held up only by a stick or a hand – or, in extreme scenarios, Minas's head. But I'd come to enjoy driving her.

'You're driving too slowly,' he complained as I steered the Lada carefully up the track.

'Well, you shouldn't have had so much raki and beer,' I said, grinning. 'Then you could drive. As it is, you'll just have to get used to it.'

'OK… Well, it's nice for someone else to drive for a change.'

It was amusing to go out to Parthenon for the evening with my hair all crazy and blonde with a summer's worth of salt and sun, skinny and tanned, the wild woman who lived at the beach. The village men were watching the football game, and we drank wine and chatted with his friends, but it all felt a bit sedate. It was strange to sleep in a bed, in a bedroom, for the first time in ages, and have an indoor shower in the morning without having to worry about my clothes blowing away. Minas's relatives made us coffee and I visited Archontoula, then we hurried back to the beach to be open for lunch.

We were still working hard but the hours were much shorter and the takings were fine now we no longer had to pay staff. It felt great to have the valley to ourselves and the days at the taverna were like a drop-in party: making food for friends, having a beer and a chat, going to the beach... In the evening, a big, yellow full moon rose over the sea and a cat tiptoed in, hoping for scraps.

Though I'd longed for the end of the summer, it was sad to see the days getting shorter. The shadow of the hills covered the beach by around five in the afternoon, and it felt late by seven thirty. There was a sense of melancholy about the prospect of closing the taverna at the end of the season. We'd have to develop a new routine, focus on fresh plans and give ourselves a rest. Minas said we could extend the roof, enclose the outside area, put in a wood-burning fire, do the olive harvest in November, maybe stay open for friends... It was a nice thought, to live here in the winter.

The person from the local authority responsible for checking on the illegal placing of umbrellas on beaches finally turned up – and started to talk very sternly to Minas until he pointed out he was the one who had lodged the complaint. 'Where were you two months ago?' he asked the official. The man told him the neighbours would get a hefty fine depending on the square metreage, but nothing would be done to stop them doing the same next year. The government needed money, Minas speculated later, so perhaps the system was to let people do illegal things and fine them.

'*Chronia polla!*'

Stamatis gave us a wonderful surprise, driving up from Pigadia in a borrowed car to sell some fish. We'd been missing him. He brought tobacco for Minas and a box of decadent cakes from the bakery in town, though he'd got hungry on the way up and eaten one. He always had a sweet tooth. Stamatis said he'd get a different helper next year, but he couldn't simply buy a new van even if he could scrape together enough money, as it needed a special licence. He would have to travel to Athens to deal with the licence; some of the campers, now back home in the city, had offered to help.

'We have our health… Health above all!' he said, cheerful as ever.

Minas asked me to prepare calamari for us all. He usually grilled it whole on the charcoal, but for a meze he told me how to slice it into rings, dip it in egg and salted flour, then deep-fry it. I made salad too, and the three of us sat down to eat together, just as we had months ago (except now with the tomatoes for the salad cut properly, of course). Stamatis said he hoped to come back before the end of September and sleep on the beach for a while, relax and enjoy days like this. We bought some of his fish to keep us going for a few days.

Now when people showed up at the taverna, Minas had time to talk to them properly – he'd often had to leave that to me during the busy days – and to experiment with mezes. He fried aubergines, and baked shrimp on the grill with cheese. A group of Greek men were so delighted with the food and the atmosphere that they bought drinks for the other tables to spread the good mood. A Danish couple had been coming every day since we introduced them to a secluded little beach reached by a path around the headland. They came for breakfast, spent all day in the sun, and returned for beers at the end of the afternoon. One afternoon, a chic-looking Italian couple arrived and asked about the road, admitting they were nervous about driving back.

'Don't worry, I have the solution!' said Minas, eyes twinkling, and they looked intrigued. He told me in Greek to bring out the raki. 'Drink this,' he said, 'and think *the road is fantastic…*' They laughed, charmed.

One morning as I prepared to drive up to the village, I heard an engine and saw what looked like a big boat in the bay, loaded with people. The big boats normally passed straight by on the way to Diafani – were they coming to us? That would be strange. Minas had told me the bigger boats didn't stop here because we didn't have a proper dock. And sure enough, when I went down to the beach, there was just a couple swimming. I had a quick dip, headed back to the taverna to knead some bread dough, then left. There were fewer but longer bookings for the rooms now, which left me with much more free time. Our latest guests arrived in hiking gear, having taken on one of the more challenging walking paths that day. I realised we could do more advertising of the rooms to hikers in the winter.

While I was cleaning the upstairs room, a couple asked to come in and look around. I showed them the old-style wooden *soufa* bed with its storage space underneath, and then, feeling cheeky, told them about the tradition that when the man behaved badly, the woman would lock him in there. The man looked a little worried.

'I'm joking!' I said.

But his wife seemed to think it might be a good idea.

It's a shame we didn't have one down at the taverna…

I took my time in the village, leaving flyers on cars and speaking to friends. While hanging up laundry I heard a shout and saw Maroukla sitting in her courtyard. I waved back, left the sheets drying on the line and wandered over. I found her down winding steps in the sunny courtyard. She asked if Minas had paid me.

Most of the money we'd made over the summer was already accounted for: Minas's bills, a monster of an electricity bill for running the fridges and freezers, the installation and monthly bills for satellite internet, materials for fixing the taverna roof and wooden walls. Anything left had to go towards fixing the roof of the *spitaki*, which Minas had promised the owner he would do in return for using it, and maintenance at the hotel; there might just be enough left to pay for my trip home.

'I have a place to live and eat and do my own work, and what we make we put back into the business.'

She seemed satisfied. 'Well, that's good, if you can do your own work. We haven't seen you for a while.' I liked that people were watching out for me.

When I drove back to the taverna, Minas was in a happy mood. There was a couple sitting at the corner table.

'We came by boat to see you!' they said.

They looked a little familiar; it turned out that Richard and Helen, an English couple, were staying at a coastal village further south and had visited Ayios Minas briefly with friends earlier in their holiday, though I hadn't met them myself – I might have smiled and said hello as I walked past. They had loved the wild, unspoiled beach and the taverna in the olive grove. They'd watched me swim around the bay and thought what a lovely way of life it must be. So for Helen's fiftieth birthday Richard had arranged an unusual surprise for her.

There was a big excursion boat that passed by here on its way north – the boat I'd seen earlier in the day. Although it had no way of docking at our beach, he had talked the captain into dropping them off close to shore. They could dive off and swim ashore, and the boat would pick them up later. Richard had brought a dry-bag to put all their valuables in – money, glasses and phones and other fragile items – and he'd tow it carefully behind him.

As the boat had drawn into the glittering blue bay, they saw the white church on top of the cliff, the shady trees, the curve of beach with just a few couples lounging here and there. Then, as they prepared to take the plunge, they saw something hurtling overhead. The captain had grabbed their bag of valuables and thrown it to shore. Thankfully, the contents were intact, and they laughed as they told the story, drinking beers and eating calamari after a memorable day.

'Shall we open that bottle of wine?' asked Minas.

His friends from Malta had brought a special bottle for us, and we opened it to share the celebration. I'd seen so many couples of all ages and nationalities linger here over lunch or dinner; the dreamy look in people's eyes as they asked if there were rooms where they could stay; and the adventurous spirit with which they borrowed sleeping bags and a tent to spend the night on the beach, listening to lapping waves, the moonlight glimmering on the water. It was a world apart: remote, hidden, pure, romantic.

Minas and I weren't that sort of couple, at least not yet – for most of the summer we'd had very little time to ourselves, in any case. Still, we'd become some sort of couple, if a slightly odd one. I'd learned that in fact Minas didn't like the beach at all, except when he threw sticks for Lisa; he certainly never swam. He didn't like fresh fish much, either – he preferred steak or burgers or chicken. He didn't appear to have any interest in walking, though that didn't bother me as I was happy to walk alone, with Lisa. We were two people with different interests who just happened to love being in that place, if for slightly different reasons; we enjoyed one another's company and cared for each other and mostly got along very well.

Minas said, 'For a Greek to end up here is crazy, especially one who doesn't like the beach or the sea or fish. But for an English woman to end up here with him… You must be crazier than me.'

❖ ❖ ❖ ❖

One dawn in the latter half of September, although the horizon was clear and deep pink there was a thick bank of cloud above, and gauzy curtains of rain falling out to sea. Then the first rainfall since May brought the rich, intense smell of spices and old wood to the valley. We gathered our things up at the intact end of the tent, put sleeping bags over our feet at the other end, which was only exposed mesh, and went back to sleep as soft raindrops and the occasional olive fell.

When I woke again, the sun was sneaking through the clouds and warming the valley. It was strange to see the ground dark from its soaking.

'We won't have a problem with dust today, at least,' said Minas.

On the other hand, it meant people were less likely to come to the beach. What's more, the rain had obviously been heavier elsewhere, as it had taken out the power. Without power, and therefore without refrigerators, it was very quiet. Minas decided to drive to town and pay the overdue electricity bill Maroukla had given me to bring down. Having no power goaded him into action, warning him what it would be like if we got cut off. He also wanted to buy a muzzle for Lisa so we could try letting her free during the day without her attacking the goats. I'd tried one before and didn't think it would work, but she might go for it if he put it on her.

There wasn't much I could do, with no water in the taps – the water pump was electric – and no lights or internet. A light rain was dripping into the terrace of the taverna through the gaps between the wooden planks of the pergola. It was raining through the ceiling of the *spitaki* too. I shut up shop and took Lisa to the beach, throwing a stick into the sea for her, then tied her up and went for a swim. The bay was pale grey and calm; a few raindrops created a beautiful pattern on the water, then it died off again and a light wind came up, the sun making the sea sparkle.

I couldn't see any goats and imagined they were sheltering, so I let Lisa free. She enjoyed racing around, sniffing everything, and came back thirsty and happy. Making a Greek coffee for myself on the gas burner, I saw that the sky remained full of grey clouds, and expected we'd have the valley to ourselves all day. I set up the smallest table in the doorway of the kitchen, with enough daylight that I could read. Lisa lay by the taverna entrance, waiting for Minas to return. There was a sound of waves dashing into shore and thunder rumbling in the distance. When I went outside I could just make out the sight of men climbing the electricity pylon at the top of the hill, working to restore the power.

Then I heard a car, and in walked another British couple who'd been here several days earlier. We stood in the doorway to the kitchen, the only dry space, and I poured them glasses of raki. They said the power was off all over the island. The thunder rumbled again, but I saw a few cars drive down the track, and people swimming. Amazingly, another group of visitors arrived, two Danish women and a Swiss man. I poured them shots of raki too, impressed that they were here on such a day. They bought beers and we had a laugh together, sitting in the rain. Then a German man arrived, had a Greek coffee and moved on to beer.

Having expected to find me forlorn and miserable on his return, Minas was astonished to hear laughter and voices. When the rain got heavier again, we all moved to the kitchen. Then an Italian couple showed up, whose friends had been here earlier in the summer and recommended the place. We were running out of space in the kitchen but, not to be deterred, Minas set up an umbrella for them over a table on the terrace.

'We're thinking of setting the place up for the winter,' he said.

They loved the idea: a beach taverna open all year.

❖ ❖ ❖ ❖

Minas tried the muzzle he'd bought for Lisa. She looked horribly humiliated, very sorry for herself, her eyes bleak. We encouraged her, saying she looked lovely and that she should go for a nice walk in it. She trotted away until she was out of reach, then writhed around on the ground until she wrenched it off. It was a nice idea.

After the rain I started to see and hear more birds around the valley, and dragonflies. In these islands, the rain always starts to bring things back to life. I did what I'd promised myself and explored the area, walking and swimming with Lisa. And when we weren't busy I did my own work in the *spitaki*. One day when the bay was deep blue with a strong wind blowing, I'd been working and sauntered down to the taverna to find every table full.

'I was just about to call you,' said Minas.

I jumped in and checked who needed what. Rolf the German from the rainy day was back, having a pork chop and beer. So was

Peter the Swedish man, who'd started coming for beers. Whenever people visited us and had a good time, Minas would say, 'They'll be back every day for sure,' and of course people often weren't, but Peter was back almost every afternoon, a reassuring presence. For a start, he made our own beer intake look more reasonable. He refused to let me take away the empties, preferring to line them up on the table. Not wanting any accidents on the road, Minas made mezes for him with chicken and peppers and cream.

The wind sent the fries flying off the plate as I carried them out. An Israeli couple said the calamari was the best they'd ever had and that they were thinking of coming to camp next summer. I overheard Minas telling people that we were doing up the *spitaki* as my office for the winter, which he'd mentioned – he had to put a new roof on anyway. Then we'd rent it to guests in summer when I had to 'balance' my work – this last bit made me smile.

'Are you hungry or thirsty or both?'

All the customers those days seemed to be hungry and thirsty. Six guys arrived on quad bikes, ordered a few beers each and then food, including a large grouper. A group of Dutch cyclists who had rented both the hotel rooms cycled down to see us and ate heartily. Some Hungarian surfers drove up from the south and, while they had a beer or two, Minas started sneakily grilling a pork chop, whetting their appetites further by raving about the surfing possibilities in the north. They ended up staying for dinner. Then a middle-aged French couple asked me, pointing at Minas, 'Is he… *chanteur*? We find him on YouTube!' They insisted on hearing a song or two, and Minas was happy to oblige.

Stamatis managed to return before September was over, with a new helper, and it was good to see him, cheery as always. He'd brought fresh tuna, which Minas filleted and fried, and we ate together with salad and fresh bread as the sun was setting. He said I was like a sister to him.

The next day, we loaned Stamatis some money towards his van repairs and bought four beautiful, large fish from him, although it was unlikely that they would all sell.

We had four tables for lunch that day.

'Would you like to see the fish?' I asked, as usual, and was astonished when everyone said yes. It must have been good karma. Three of the couples ordered a fish to share. The fourth ordered calamari, feeling the last fish was too big for two people, though they eyed the other tables jealously. Then an Austrian couple who came regularly arrived and were delighted to find the perfect fish for their last dinner here of the year.

They ordered a coffee after their meal, then asked Minas with a smile, 'Is it your birthday?'

'Of course!' said Minas, grinning.

As lunch wound up, all the fish sold, I finished a mound of dishes in the kitchen and came back out, ready for a swim.

'It's been a good day!' I said to Minas.

'And there are four more people coming up...' he replied.

'Really?'

He howled with laughter. 'No! Wouldn't that be good, though?!'

I rolled my eyes.

I picked up my towel and went over to the door, heading down to the beach, then looked back and said nonchalantly, 'Oh, you mean those four people?' And there were.

I woke next morning in the cosy tent to another sunny morning with a cool breeze, and looked through the window at the olive trees and the sea, the pink and orange clouds. I had recently found the original bag the tent came in, and the label that called it a 'well-ventilated dome'. It made me laugh – one whole end of the tent was just mesh, the outer skin shredded like paper by summer sun and wind. As soon as I unzipped the side, Lisa poked her head through then came flying in and lay on top of me.

After a swim and breakfast, I worked for a while at my desk outside the *spitaki* in the shade of the olive tree, glimpsing the sea sparkling in the distance through its branches, while Minas researched parts for broken machinery. I could easily see if someone arrived or if Minas needed me. I would go up to Olympos to clean both of the rooms that day – it should be the last changeover of the season.

The village was clear and bright in the sunshine, impossibly vertical from certain angles. And it was eerily quiet, the tour groups suddenly gone, gift shops closed. I noticed two young boys with school bags and realised the children must be back at school. Pressing laundry for the rooms, I was as usual being hasty and burning my fingers on the sheets hot from the steam press. My hands were recovering from the summer, though my fingerpads were still crisscrossed with cuts. It had been a summer of getting my fingers burned – fire and ice in more ways than one.

I didn't have much enthusiasm for cleaning rooms again, but the previous guests had left them nicely and it didn't take long, and it was always satisfying to see how pretty the rooms looked with everything in place and the sheets and towels arranged. And thanks to the rain, the hotel's red-painted woodwork didn't need washing. Old Kalliopi waved to me from her kafeneio as I left. Nikos' wife Maria, sitting outside Parthenon doing lacework, called out '*Yeia sou Evgenia!*' When I asked what beautiful thing she was making, she just shrugged and smiled shyly, 'Oh, just something to pass the time…' As I passed by,

Foula usually shouted '*Filenada mou!*', 'My friend!' She wasn't sitting outside on the steps and I missed her.

When people asked what our plans were now that the season was drawing to a close, I mentioned we might be staying open a while. A couple of people said it would be terrible in the winter, cold, with no people... But I'd had enough hot, busy days and looked forward to peace and quiet. Minas thought we'd get locals coming to fish, to watch the football away from the village... Whether it would be sustainable, who knew?

Driving back, I thought about what to eat later: maybe a Greek salad, chips and tzatziki. I still needed to put a bit of weight back on. There were no cars at the beach, but the young electrician who'd given me a ride early in the summer had returned with his mate and his truck was parked behind the taverna. It was good to see them again. I left the boys to drink beer and went to the beach with Lisa, had a swim and dried off in the sun and the wind. Lisa sunbathed next to me, licking my hand to make me stroke her. Then I walked up to the little house, where the bed was heaped with cotton blankets and sleeping bags. Tiny pebbles had fallen from the ceiling but it had survived the earth tremor that Minas now blamed for destroying the kitchen ceiling a few weeks earlier. If we stayed open in the winter, I'd definitely need this as my own space.

At sunset, as always, there were beautiful colours in the bay, metallic blue and silver-green water, and the wind spreading ripples out to sea, making tiny waves. It was hard to believe there was no more rushing around to be done, getting up to clean and make breakfasts for campers, dashing to fix rooms and back to help with the lunchtime crowd, waking up in the night, dreaming that there were customers waiting to be served. It had finished for this summer at least.

I'd have a trip back to Tilos in October while the weather was still beautiful. I'd buy gifts from Rigopoula to take to my friends Ed and Anna. I'd enjoy the lovely red-sand beaches of my home island and the ease of being able to stroll to a shop to buy food from my old house in the village, before returning. I wasn't ready to leave the taverna by the sea yet.

AFTER THE SUMMER

In early November, the church of Ayios Minas on the cliffs celebrated the saint's day with a religious service and a social gathering, and I walked up there to see it. Friends insisted I take some blessed bread. It was Minas's name day, but he stayed at the taverna, and a few people went down there to wish him '*Chronia polla*'.

Most people visiting the valley now were locals, here to check on their land or animals, occasionally to hunt or fish, and a few stopped in for coffee or a beer and meze. Technically we were open, because we were mostly living there, but we didn't do anything special to advertise the fact or keep too much in stock, and it was Minas's domain now, with no need for me to help. If a group of friends from Diafani wanted to come, they would call in advance to check he was open and tell him what they wanted to eat.

It was autumn, the season of ripe pomegranates and mandarins. Gentle, warm winds came from the sea, and the waves were boisterous enough for us to hear them from the taverna day and night. For the cool nights, Minas built a temporary fireplace for the newly enclosed taverna terrace, and sometimes cooked over it for us.

One day he went to collect olive wood for the fire and on his return presented me with a couple of myrtle branches. The wild myrtle berries, *myrta*, had a strong, spicy citrus flavour and a sourness that was beautifully countered by heaps of creamy yoghurt. Having grown up picking wild blackberries, fresh berries were something I'd missed in my Greek island diet so far. Sophia and Evgenia, visiting regularly now to look after their goats, told me they ate the berries with raisins. Sophia also showed me the *skinokarpo*, tiny red peppercorn-like berries on the mastic bushes that turned black when ripe. I picked one and crushed it between my fingers, releasing a peppery aroma. Minas suggested we bake a few into the fresh bread with onion.

I'd looked forward to learning about the olive harvest, and spent a few enjoyable days up a wooden ladder pulling olives down from the branches. Minas and Sophia showed me how to separate the good fruit from bad, and I loved the different shades, from black to purple to brown and green, in the gathered heaps. We put them in fresh water for a few days before making a brine to keep them in. Minas picked thyme, *thymari*, to use when cooking meat, and also when preserving the olives.

Since we weren't tied to the taverna, one day when the weather forecast showed fierce winds and heavy rain we drove up to the village to stay in the rooms for a couple of nights. In the evening, Archontoula offered us wine with a meze of chickpea soup, bread and olives. I ate and then went over to the post office/souvlaki shop. It seemed to be closed but there was a key in the wooden door, so I opened it. Yiannis with his grizzled beard was inside, feet up on the counter and reclined so far back that I thought he was asleep, and a wood fire roared in the corner hearth. He told me which pile of mail my parcel was in, and which pile was today's; these little things made me feel that I was becoming part of village life.

Back at Archontoula's, Minas had ordered more wine and was getting tipsier, yet accepted my suggestion that we not drink the fourth half-litre but take it home. I woke up in the night and needed to open the window, so used was I to fresh air from sleeping outside. It felt too quiet with no sound of waves.

Minas woke up early and was heading into town to get petrol, maybe see the bank; the internet company had found an old outstanding debt of his, another to add to the list. I saw him looking at the view from the balcony, the clouds on the mountain. 'I haven't been here for a while, and had forgotten how nice it is.'

I walked the footpath down to the riverbed, finding myrtle and mint and a crab. When I came back, I met Rigopoula and her husband Yiannis, who insisted on giving me a slice of the cake he'd just baked.

'You must be a good person,' he said, 'because no-one in the village has anything bad to say about you and it's a difficult village.' They taught me the local dialect word for gossip, *koureto*.

'Maybe I need to stay a bit longer, give them something to talk about,' I quipped.

The idea of gossip had never bothered me, though Minas had always warned me that the village ladies saw everything and word would get back to his mother in the city if, for example, we didn't sweep the courtyard of her house. When he came to the village and got into conversation with someone, it would often start with a calculation of how they were related, second cousins connected by marriage or some such thing. And anyone from the village, relative or not, would feel obliged to offer an opinion on how he was organising his life. People always said to him, 'You're clever, but *valeh mialo*, use your head!'

So I could see why the beach was a necessary escape from scrutiny and judgement; a place where he could be a singer – not of traditional local songs but American rock – and be a little crazy and unconventional. As for me, an outsider, I was somewhat exempt from the rules of village life – a local woman couldn't have gone to the kafeneio alone – but I still felt a sense of release when I got back to the beach in the middle of nowhere, with nothing but the sea and the trees and the goats. Just as it was a place of escape for visitors, the empty valley was a place where we could be ourselves.

Back down at the taverna, now that it was quiet, I mostly sat at a table in a sunny corner to do my writing and editing work, looking out into the olive grove and listening to the birds.

'Can you edit me?' said Minas, watching me before he disappeared inside to create something interesting for dinner. 'New recipe – no guarantees!' He tested new ideas for the menu; calamari stuffed with brown rice and spinach was a definite winner. He sometimes went up to the one of the local villages, Olympos or Spoa, to fix someone's fridge. He often wouldn't ask for payment from the older villagers and would return instead with fresh goats' cheese or milk or bread that he'd been given, and one time some pomegranate juice that was intriguingly fizzy.

We went into town together and I got to know the suppliers. We invested in new pillows for the hotel rooms, and I found fitted sheets. We tried some local sausages that we decided would be a great hit next summer, and different wine. We came up with ideas. I'd noticed that in the busy days of summer, we couldn't really spare the few minutes it took to fill a wine carafe from the tap on the box of chilled wine. So we found some rather nice-looking screw-top bottles, decanted wine into them and kept a stack constantly on hand in the fridge. Unfortunately, it made it even easier to drink an extra half-litre in the evening... But if we felt like staying up late, drinking a little too much wine and dancing to music on the terrace, we did.

The only one of us who didn't like winter much was Lisa, who missed her huge feasts of bones and chips, and who was terrified by the sounds of gunshots when hunters came; we'd been lucky that hunting was prohibited on Tilos. She didn't much like the dancing, either. Yet when I took a trip to England to see my family, over Christmas and into January, I left her with Minas and she was delighted to drive around in the Lada with him, taking over the front seat. He spent time with Pavlos fixing the roof of the little house, and in the evenings he trained Lisa to offer one paw and then the other – a trick that would make her even more popular and win her more treats.

In London, Tim and Alison took me for dinner and we finally had the leisurely conversation we'd never had time for over the summer. In a hardware shop near my mum's house, I found keysafes for the hotel rooms. We'd attach them to the wall and give guests the combination to access and replace their keys. It should be simpler for everyone. I had notes of other things that we could do better, from using bins for the rubbish bags at the taverna to checking the water level daily.

It was wonderful to return in mid-January to sunshine, deep blue sea and the vibrant green of pine trees and mastic bushes. The weather was mostly serene, as were things between me and Minas. I fell asleep listening to the waves coming into shore – I think this is when I became addicted to the sea – and woke with the sun. At other times, there were fierce, biting winds and I couldn't walk up the track without being afraid of being blown over. More and more anemones, mauve and pink, carpeted the path to the beach, and under the olive trees were lush green patches of grass with sprays of bright yellow Bermuda buttercups.

I swam and walked, exploring the hills and valleys covered in thick bush and pine trees that went on forever. My walking boots were a little tattered from being left out in the salt air and sun all summer. I saw pristine pebble beaches and sheer cliffs, riverbeds leading to little old stone houses with wooden doors, ruined shepherds' huts, fields and fields of olive trees. Lisa and I could walk for hours without encountering anyone, returning when the clouds were pink in a dusky pale blue sky. In the evening, the only sounds were the sea and the hiss of wood on the open fire. I truly started to feel a sense of belonging. It was the kind of winter I'd hoped for. Minas and I were both quite self-contained, doing our own thing, yet we had fun together and enjoyed one another's company and I felt content.

One afternoon I had a few hours when work wasn't pressing, and decided to walk the first track up to the road, along the road and down the second track – maybe nine kilometres in total. When Minas said he'd come with me, I nearly fell over with the shock. Reaching the road, we encountered Sophia and Evgenia looking for stray goats, and when they saw Minas walking they thought our car must have broken down… But he even seemed to enjoy it.

They invited us to their farm the next day on the other side of the ridge. We drove up and then with Evgenia and Georgia we had a leisurely hike down through the rocky river valley at Argoni. Pavlos joined us for a big meal cooked by Sophia – their own goat in tomato sauce with spaghetti and heaps of their own cheese, accompanied by red wine made by Minas's uncle Antonis. We watched the orange sun descend in a clear blue sky between the jagged silhouettes of sheer mountains.

Life had changed in a good way since I came to Karpathos. I felt welcomed into this exceptional community and it was time to embrace this next chapter. In any case, it seemed illogical to continue paying rent in Tilos if I wasn't living there; keeping on the house was cluttering my life in a way I didn't need. In March I went back again and packed up my things, then arranged to get furniture and boxes shipped over.

I saw so many friends over those days on Tilos, visiting favourite places in between bouts of cleaning the house and giving things away. It was difficult as the island meant a lot to me. My neighbour Michaelia was sad at first that I was letting the house go, but she understood when I explained and said, in her slightly scolding way, that it would be good for me to settle down. My landlord Antonis said more pragmatically, 'I know you're an *eleftheros anthropos,*' a free person, 'and anytime you want to come back, you'll be welcome.' Irini asked, more pragmatically still, for my pots of parsley.

I loved that ramshackle old house, perhaps a bit more without all my junk in it. I sat there alone one night, thinking how wonderfully peaceful it was. Was it always that tranquil? Suddenly I remembered. I'd left Lisa with Minas. If she'd been with me, she'd have been barking at every neighbour's footfall and every passing cat. And Menelaos, if he'd been walking by, would have cursed at her perhaps... And I'd have been shouting at her and running up the steps to bring her inside.

My friend Ed, who'd looked after the house in my absence, came to help me with the four bags and the box I was taking on the ferry. Although he always had plenty of company, a few good friends of his had left the island over the last few years. As he drove me down to the port, he must have rolled his eyes listening to me saying once again, 'What am I thinking, leaving Tilos?!'

We pulled up outside Remezzo, the café-bar on the port, to wait for the boat.

'Vodka tonic,' said Ed, and it seemed a good idea.

I heard my name and as I went inside to order drinks, I saw Pavlos the bus driver. We'd exchanged hellos over the last few days, but I guessed that maybe he'd forgotten my name, seeing me without Lisa, and he'd just said, '*Yeia sou...*' This time, he remembered, and shouted out his habitual greeting for me: '*Yeia sou* Jennifer Lopez!'

❖ ❖ ❖ ❖

On a hot, sunny day in late March, I walked the old footpath from Olympos to the higher plateau of Avlona. The terraced fields glowed a vivid green, the houses bright white against the severe grey of the mountain. Minas was helping his uncle trim the vines and then insisted on driving me to an even higher valley to see the wild white peonies that blossomed just for those few weeks.

When a spring thunderstorm came, a deluge of rain knocked out the power temporarily and left roads broken and covered in rockslides. Staying in Olympos, I was astonished by the noise of streams rushing down the mountains around the village, a gushing river filling the valley and washing down so much earth that it changed the colour of the sea, while gorgeous waterfalls appeared. Sophia, who had the cafc-bar at the entrance to the village, was weaving rushes into crosses for the church.

Minas cleared the building rubble from the unfinished space below the hotel rooms and made it into a laundry room with a washing line so I could leave sheets to dry when I wasn't there. It would eventually become another hotel room but Minas could only progress with it when the cash was available. I caught up on all the laundry, sorted it and put it away in a wardrobe in the new laundry room, along with the toiletries and everything else needed during changeovers. That summer, we'd be better organised.

When the sun came out again, the light was intense, the sky a stunningly clear blue. We drove back down to Ayios Minas, where the riverbed that functioned as the road to the beach in summer had also turned into a river, bordered by fragrant pines and overhung by branches heavy with yellow blossoms. Lisa loved the rock pools.

Thanks to all the rain, abundant flowers of different types appeared every day in every colour in the bright green fields and dark green hills. In the valley we saw the occasional hoopoe, Bonelli's eagle, falcon and kestrel. People brought us bags of artichokes that grew around the edges of their fields and were now in season. Archontoula had been preparing artichokes when I'd first arrived, just before Easter the year before, and now I learned to trim around the hearts, boil them with lemon and salt, and cover them with *ladolemono* – olive oil and lemon juice.

I walked down to the beach for a swim, and hadn't got very far out when a white fishing boat appeared around the headland and turned into the bay: it was Stamatis, on his first visit since September. I waved and went to fetch Minas, and Stamatis handed us a keepnet full of flapping *menoula*. We put some tables together and grilled the fish on the barbecue. So much had happened in the last year since we'd first done this.

From now on, with the weather warming up and visitors beginning to come back to the island, we'd mostly stay down at the taverna. But on Easter Saturday I went back up to the village with Minas, who was helping his uncle Nick for a few evenings at the taverna. I made friends with a couple of visitors who offered me a drink, and the evening flew by as we listened to traditional music being played in the square and firecrackers going off as people passed by towards the church. When the service ended, from the taverna we saw people pouring out of the church and we went to greet friends with the customary words *Christos Anesti*, Christ is Risen. I now felt so much more part of this. Minas and I followed a group of young people from the city to Archtontoula's to offer Easter greetings. To break the fast of Lent there was *patsa*, morsels of goat's stomach cooked in an egg-and-lemon broth. As the young city people nervously pushed bits of tripe around their plates, something about seeing them squirm – plus the large quantity of wine we'd drunk – made Minas and me dig in.

Back at the taverna early next morning, we started preparing for the day. The weather couldn't have been more beautiful: not a breeze or a cloud to bother the blue sky. I kneaded bread dough and left it to rise while Minas lit charcoal and attached the whole goat, slaughtered at the top of the valley a couple of nights earlier, to the spit. He'd made tzatziki and *melitzanosalata*, aubergine salad. We cleaned and organised, then I went for a swim. The sea was flat and calm, the pebbles and sand too hot to walk on for the first time this year. Lisa announced the first guests, the usual Distant Early Warning signal. We were expecting the Swiss walking group that came every Easter, some staying at our hotel rooms – and as they hiked down the track, her barks accompanied them. Meanwhile, I walked up the riverbed and noticed that the overhanging trees had shed their little pom-poms overnight, leaving the ground dusted with gold, and the yellow broom flowers were now smelling sweet – I picked a few, thinking we could decorate the tables with them. The taverna looked good with its bright blue tables and chairs and wooden walls, surrounded by green fields and olive trees. The food was ready just as the sun began to drop towards the hilltops.

I felt a sense of completeness living here. It had now been a year: the last six months had been a big reward for the work of the previous six. That's what so many islanders' lives were like. In the corner of the terrace we'd hung sprigs of oregano, *rigani*, from the wooden beams to dry; it was something I usually did in Tilos and Minas had agreed it would be good for salads. I was contributing my touch to the taverna. The corner had a bookshelf with my books, and a painting of Odysseus given to me by Yiannis, Rigopoula's husband, with a quotation from Cavafy's poem 'Ithaka': *Hope that the road is long, full of adventure.*

The sea was getting warmer, swallows were flitting overhead and families of baby partridges waddled through the fields. Summer was around the corner and it was beginning to get too hot to walk far into the hills. Bookings were coming in for the rooms – though I made sure we didn't accept any single-night reservations for the middle of summer; that couldn't happen unless we had someone on site. As charter flights began, a few people arrived from across Europe. I made semolina halva, and apple cake with olive oil, drizzled with local honey, to offer to guests early in the season while we had time; and we had a few of our own olives to offer too.

A couple walked down the track in the afternoon, sat by the sea and then came up to drink some wine and decided to stay for an early dinner. We learned their names were Lella and Pierangelo. Minas poured them raki for his birthday, then Lella sang 'Happy Birthday'.

'Darling, let me tell you something,' said Minas, his arm around her. 'It's not really my birthday. I told you it was my birthday because I wanted to buy you a drink.'

He sang a Greek song for her and they sang Beatles numbers together and we laughed and danced. It was one of the things so special about running a taverna here; when we met people like that, it was like making new friends. Finally, we hugged and kissed goodbye and Minas drove them up to the road, Lella insisting she was sorry that she'd interrupted his birthday.

❖ ❖ ❖ ❖

A few months earlier, Minas had done some research at the council offices in town and learned that he and the neighbours were each entitled to attend a municipal auction for the licence to put umbrellas on the beach. I'd gone along too and found it interesting. Apparently, if a beach had a business directly behind it, they had first refusal, but otherwise the umbrella rights to every beach were up for grabs by the highest bidder.

The neighbours hadn't looked too happy to see us on the appointed morning at the council auction room, realising that Minas would be bidding against them. He and I and Pavlos had agreed to pool some money and see if we could win the rights, so that Minas could choose to put umbrellas on the beach or not. The bidding quickly went into thousands of euros and, having agreed on a maximum amount, we eventually bowed out; the neighbours had won, but seemed furious that we'd competed and made them pay more than they'd hoped.

Meanwhile, one day in spring we'd had a visit from a man called Manolis from the island of Crete who worked with *kalami*, bamboo, building everything from beach umbrellas and pergolas to little houses. He showed us photographs and said he was thinking of coming back with his team to see if they could pick up work. We thought it looked good, and Minas gave him some names to contact. A few weeks later, we needed a favour from him. A strange rattle in the Lada turned out to be a bearing in the gearbox ready to quit, and the cost of fixing it seemed too much to spend on something held together by rust and good fortune. Minas found a replacement old Lada Niva on Crete and called Manolis to ask him to check it out; it was declared fine. Cash was tight for Minas since he'd stayed on the island all winter without much income, but I could pay for it now and we'd make the amount back in a few days over the summer. Our new friend would bring it with him when he and his team arrived for work.

The evening Manolis was due to arrive we drove to Diafani and had a drink while we waited. The old ship *Prevelis* was due to arrive at eight, but actually showed its face sometime close to ten. Minas drove the new old Lada off the boat and I had a few minutes to acquaint myself with it before setting off to lead the convoy, Minas in the faulty old Lada and the team from Crete in their truck. As someone who had refused to drive a car for twenty years, I'd come a long way, I thought as I drove up the winding road from the port in the dark, across the ridge and down the dirt track with mountain on one side and sheer drop on the other.

For a couple of weeks in May, the team based themselves at the taverna, enjoying fresh fish and local goat for dinner. One gorgeous night I looked around the terrace: with the guys from Crete, the local fishermen, a couple from Austria, music playing and meat roasting on a spit, and of course Lisa wandering around from table to table, it felt like the coolest taverna in Karpathos.

In between doing other jobs, the guys built a few bamboo teepees which we thought looked magnificent: temporary structures of local, natural materials tucked unobtrusively in a corner of the beach, sheltering against the wind and with a door looking straight out to sea. After the guys moved on, we put mattresses and pillows inside. The previous year, people had borrowed sleeping bags from us and camped on the beach and had a great experience, but they hadn't always slept well. These provided the perfect amount of comfort in a wild place; people could stay for dinner and drinks without worrying about driving, have a morning swim then come to us for breakfast and a shower. When my family and friends came to visit – as several were planning to in June and July – they'd have a place to stay. The teepees soon became my favourite place to sleep, too. Before long, everyone who drove down to the beach was taking pictures of the teepees, sharing photos, asking if they could rent them…

Minas had reassured me that he'd talked to people and we wouldn't have any trouble. But he was wrong. Because with July came the neighbours and another bout of the taverna wars. They happen all over Greece where there are rival tavernas, but the people of the north of Karpathos can bring their own special zeal to fights. And if people were using a teepee, they didn't need to rent a beach umbrella…

First, we had a visit from the port police, who said it was illegal to build even a temporary structure on a beach without a licence; and then from the building regulations people too. There would be fines to pay at the end of the summer, and the teepees would have to come down. There was no proof that the neighbours had instigated this, but it seemed possible because we also had a visit from the tax department at the end of July. And then a policeman arrived to investigate a complaint made by the neighbour against me.

I was shaken. We sat down together at one of the tables and he told me not to worry, then he consulted his notes.

'She says you have been bothering the customers of her umbrellas and taking business away from her,' he stated.

If I hadn't been so nervous, I could have laughed. I explained, 'But I never go near the umbrellas except just to say hello to people I know. I'd be afraid to.'

'Afraid of what?'

'Well, her husband punched Minas last year, and then he sent threats.' Then I told him about an incident a few weeks earlier. Her husband had been putting up a sign to their taverna right in the middle of a path that led to ours. I was in a bikini walking back from the beach at the time, and it was awkward to get around the sign. 'He thrust his spade at me and said, "If you touch my sign, I'll kill you." The way he said it, it was really unnerving.'

'I see,' said the policeman. 'Would you like to make a complaint?'

I smiled and said no, and thanked him. The policeman was kind, and when he realised that the complaint was groundless he took his notes and left and that was the end of the matter. My friends in Olympos said not to worry about it – it was part of running a business. But I didn't want to live like this.

Debts had also continued to emerge every time we were getting on an even keel. I was always trying to simplify my life, but here it seemed impossible: cash register, taxes, accountant, car, car repair, insurance, staff, mattresses, loans… And a few things had happened that made me feel less comfortable at the beach. I was no longer sure about life here. I was no longer sure Minas and I were the right sort of couple. It was awful for us both for a while. It was still difficult to go, but it became impossible to stay. At least for now, I had to get away.

I left one early August night with Lisa. We walked an hour up the track in the dark and then, as the sun rose, we walked hours along the road to Olympos, where we surprised a couple rounding up goats. We then walked the footpath to Diafani, from where I took the ferry that night. My body was exhausted but I had to do it to numb the pain of leaving. Poor Lisa also needed time to recover from that.

❖ ❖ ❖ ❖

I looked for a place on Tilos to rent. At first, I missed the dramatic beauty of north Karpathos. But Tilos welcomed me back and gradually

I saw friends and went to some of my favourite beaches and relaxed, and remembered why I loved this island, too.

I found myself missing Minas a bit. He might be impossible but he was still loveable. Eventually, we talked and I promised to go back just to finish the season, and he promised to make it easier for me.

Despite everything, I was happy to return to Ayios Minas, to smell the pine trees and see the blue glittering sea and the olive trees filling the valley. At the taverna, the shower door was banging in the wind as usual. Minas said there were things we could do to make things better – we could turn part of the hotel back into a house, and I could live there. But I'd have missed the beach.

When I went to Olympos to say goodbye and talked to people in the village about the problems we'd had with the other taverna, everyone had a story of something similar. Someone told me, 'I'm from here and I'm not embarrassed to say it – there are bad people here.'

But they didn't seem bad. I sat in Parthenon one day and Nikos played the lyra – softly at first, gradually growing in strength. 'I play and forget everything,' he said. 'You hear it and you don't.'

I went to the traditional bakery, where Kalliopi lifted pastries out of the wood-burning oven built into the hillside. 'Do you have anything sweet?' I asked.

'Me!'

I had hugs and kisses from Georgia and Evgenia and Sophia. There were tears in my eyes as I told them I'd be back soon.

In some ways, perhaps it could have been a rite of passage, it made me even more part of the community to have endured the taverna wars. But there were other reasons too. I needed more calm in my life. I returned to Tilos, to a place I'd arranged to rent for the winter by the sea in the port of Livadia. I missed the sound of the wind in the trees, the wilds of Ayios Minas. *Damn me for missing it...* Over the next few months I decided to put things in motion to try to buy a permanent place of my own. I needed my own space.

I'd stayed a year and a half longer than I'd originally expected when I booked those first few days in Olympos. I felt privileged to have had the experience; it was an important episode of my life, one that I wanted to remember with pleasure. I also hoped to keep a connection. The next year, I returned to Ayios Minas with Lisa and spent September there writing and swimming, occasionally helping out and seeing old friends, while Minas cooked for me. I continued to help with his room bookings remotely for the next couple of years, very happy not to be there when mix-ups happened. My wooden table, my desk for my first years on Tilos, became the VIP table in the corner of the taverna on music days.

'You helped make the taverna what it is,' Minas said to me.

The taverna helped make me what I am too, part of my Greek island evolution. A couple of years later, I luckily found a home in Tilos in a tranquil, windy bay surrounded by hills, where I could sit at my desk and see the sun glinting on the sea, and then take a break and jump in the water just as I did back at Ayios Minas. I would still spend the hottest days of summer sleeping outside, listening to the sound of the waves. And the coldest nights of winter by a wood-burning fire, sipping wine.

One day, when the hills were glowing with the last of the sun, I walked down to the sea to clean some fresh sardines I'd bought from the fisherman. A couple from Germany passed by — people I'd got to know at Ayios Minas, who also spent time on Tilos every year.

'Do you have your own restaurant now?!' they joked, knowing I lived just back from the sea. 'Is there food for two more?'

I remembered the good times wistfully, though at that moment I was glad not to have my own taverna. The experience wouldn't have been the same anywhere else, without the wild, raw, natural simplicity of Ayios Minas. Or without the force of nature that is Minas himself. He kept promising to come and visit me in Tilos, but he never did. He likes his world.

We continue to inspire each other from afar and he still makes me laugh.

'They'll make a movie of our story,' he told me. 'And we'll go to Hollywood, and they'll say *Oh, he's so short… He seemed so much taller in the book.*'

Now read an excerpt from Jen Barclay's account of her travels through the deserted places of the Dodecanese in *Wild Abandon*.

THE MAKER AND
BREAKER OF FORTUNES

Nisyros

The catamaran pulls away swiftly and I am left alone on the harbour. A few people were waiting to embark as the ferry pulled in, but now there's just me and Lisa and a delivery of boxes. I stand and enjoy the moment, the silence on the quay and the thrill of being the only person arriving on Nisyros on this calm winter day.

I've been visiting this island on and off for well over a decade, and I have stayed many times here at Mandraki. I love the sea wall with painted wooden balconies facing out over crashing waves, the clifftop monastery of our Lady of the Cave, the narrow winding alleys strewn with plant pots and overhung with washing lines. Through the summer it is busy with day trippers from Kos. Today there's no-one, and in any case I'm heading elsewhere.

My phone rings and a car approaches along the empty dock. Yiannis, my host, has come to meet me. With short dark hair and a beard, he's local and I'd guess in his late thirties, calm and genuine in his welcome. His friend from Athens has longer, straight hair and a slighter build and is delighted with Lisa. We drive to the bakery where I stock up on bread and pastries while the others head off to do banking and buy cigarettes. An old man is selling olives from the back of a truck, so I buy half a kilo. Back in the car, we set off for the village of Emborio.

While Tilos on a map is a ragged tilde, indented with promontories and inlets, Nisyros, being a volcano shaped by its eruptions, is almost round with few protuberances and barely any natural harbour. The road hugs the rocky coast for a few kilometres, following the curve of the island. Then, turning off at a junction, we start to meander up the slope, zigzagging higher. The old farming terraces on either side of us are thickly green, scattered liberally with flowers, and Yiannis points high up towards the ridge where we are heading, the white almond blossom so bright it seems to glint in the sunshine that is shyly emerging from the clouds. The car strains up the final stretch and we park on a slope just below the village. Emborio is built on the rim of the volcano, hundreds of metres above the sea and overlooking the caldera, the hollow, cauldron-like centre of the island.

As its name – like the English 'emporium' – suggests, in Roman times Emborio was a centre of trade. It continued to prosper through the Middle Ages and into the Turkish era. A century ago, the biggest village on the island, it had 2,500, maybe 3,000 residents – until an earthquake hit in 1933, also devastating Kos. World War II took its toll, too, and by 1950, the population of the village had dropped to two or three hundred people. Now the permanent residents number just seventeen.

Some houses have been bought and restored by outsiders, says Yiannis, mostly people from France and other parts of Greece, who visit for a few weeks or months a year. For more than a decade he and his brother and sister have run Apiria, the taverna by the church, and now rent out houses. In winter, theirs is the only taverna; with so few residents, it's surprising there's anything at all. We climb up an alleyway of stone steps, passing empty ruins and the former village school, before reaching a restored house of dark grey stone. The door is stiff from the rain, but with a shove it opens on to a magical bedroom with the stone arches, stone walls and stone ceiling of traditional Nisyrian houses. Stone is not a scarce commodity, clearly. The building is at least a hundred years old, says

Yiannis, which means it survived the earthquake of 1933 – making me feel a little more comfortable about the huge slabs of stone above my bed.

He hands me the keys and leaves to do his work. The decor is spare and stylish, with smooth-finished grey concrete and neutral cottons, old wooden furniture, IKEA cutlery stored in an antique icebox. Despite its contemporary touches, I am delighted to find I have neither phone signal nor Wi-Fi. I stand on the terrace, ruined walls in small fields to either side, the land dropping away beyond the edge of the ridge. The only sound is the buzzing of insects, and a dog barking. This is the last inhabited house at our end of the village. Having completed the bare essentials of settling in, I follow overgrown stone steps until the view opens up to reveal the flat caldera floor far below: the green winter fields of the plain, and white craters in the distance.

The caldera of Nisyros sits one hundred metres above sea level with lava domes rising all around to almost seven hundred metres, forming the rim where I'm standing. It is the youngest active volcano in Greece, none of its rocks more than 150,000 years old; an eruption just fifteen thousand years ago covered the existing land in another layer of pumice and ash. The last known eruptions were in the 1870s and 1880s. Today the volcano is scientifically monitored for variations such as increasing temperatures and surface cracks. This volcanic activity makes the island, at just forty-one square kilometres one of the smallest in the Dodecanese, uniquely dramatic and ever-changing.

The crater known as Stephanos is a cauldron within the caldera. Steep-sided, circular, like a vast cooking pot 180 metres in radius and 30 metres deep, it was formed six thousand years ago by super-hot liquid surging from the earth and blasting the rock away. The white, viscous liquid has cooled and hardened in the bottom of the pot, forming a thick crust, but under the surface it still boils. I have stood several times down there on the white dust of the crater, where vapour rises wispily from hissing, gurgling canary-yellow openings; as I lean in close, momentarily blinded by the steam, the hint of sulphur from the fumaroles transports me to a more elemental world. I get a sense of walking closer to the earth here, to the raw stuff it is made of. The steam, the mud, the formation of fine, fragile sulphur crystals – this rare glimpse of the planet as a living being is humbling.

It was hundreds of metres above this caldera one windy evening in 2015 that I first started thinking about the deserted places of the Dodecanese. Surrounded by warm orange light as the sun went down, I heard a cow lowing. My friend and I had climbed up the steps from Nikia, the other village on the rim of the caldera, and I contemplated the blue and white chapel, surreal in its perfection, dedicated in 2010 by a Nisyrian of New York. We had also visited the monastery of Panayia Kyra, destroyed in the earthquake of 1933 and rebuilt two years later by a brotherhood of Nisyrians in America. In the caldera, we'd seen abandoned farms: threshing circles, water cisterns and stone houses littered with animal bones.

The full moon was bright and yellow against a dusky blue sky as we drove by scooter to Emborio, where cats leapt across the alleys from one roof to another. Of the two half-empty villages that faced one another on the rim of the caldera, one – Nikia – had been endowed with the wealth of those who left for America, while the other – Emborio – seemed mostly dark and crumbling.

It struck me powerfully then that so many islanders left their rural existence for such a different, urban life on the other side of the world. But while science may reassure us today that the volcano is stable, a century ago a disastrous earthquake could have been enough to persuade people to leave. Just twenty years after the 1933 earthquake, another in 1953 led to further decline in the population of Nisyros. The effect was similar on Santorini, another volcanic island in the Cyclades just to the west, where an earthquake in 1956 also resulted in a wave of emigration. In a documentary about it called *5:12*, the old people interviewed say that after they saw houses turn to dust and people killed, from then on there was a fear of the volcano. It finished off a farming way of life that was already in decline.

The population of Nisyros has remained around a thousand for the last few decades, while the Nisyrians in the USA number around twelve thousand. One of them, John Catsimatidis, left the island as a baby with his parents in 1948, grew up in Harlem and worked in a grocery store, and is now one of the richest men in America.

This winter day, the sun is now shining and according to the forecast today is the warmest day of the week, so I have my sights set not on the interior of the island but its shoreline – and a particular beach. I stride the empty, open, curving road around the high rim of the caldera, the sea an inviting deep blue far below, the fields all green grass dotted with flowers, oak trees and spiky euphorbia bushes blossoming bright yellow. Eventually I reach the track that will take me hundreds of metres down to the shore. A man is securing a fence and I assume the goats on the road are his; I ask if I should keep the dog away, but he says, 'Not at all,' and shoos them off.

The track zigzags down, changes for a while to a path of white pumice, then to red and black pumice that feels crisp underfoot. Finally there's a scramble through sand and scrub, amid lavender bushes and olive trees, to the wind-sculpted milk-chocolate beach falling away into clear sea. I swim and then dry off on the warm, coarse sand, grains of black, red and grey. The sun will disappear behind the ridge soon and I can't linger, sadly. I risk a nerve-wracking pull up a sheer cliff using Lisa's straining on the lead to help with upward momentum, a more direct route up to the path that leads to the road.

The light is already fading as I return along the high ridge to Emborio. I see one car, one motorbike, and one black cow with very sharp-looking horns, pencil points sticking out of its head, refusing to budge from the roadside. I veer off into a sloping field to look at an abandoned square stone building with narrow slits for windows. Inside there's a deep, bath-like structure, its walls smoothly plastered white. A year before, I saw something similar beside a track among the farms above Mandraki; the drain hole at the front leading into a stone bowl made me think it might be a wine press. I pause to see a few other deserted buildings. The temperature has dropped so when I get back to the house I find the hot water switch, make Lisa some dinner, crawl under the duvet and sleep until it's time for the taverna to open.

I hear the high bleeps of scops owls. Outside, it's pitch-black and I realise that although my mobile phone is useless for making calls here, it's essential as a torch to light my way down the uneven old steps until I reach streetlights. I'm early so I walk around the village, seeing few lights on; some houses are derelict, some restored but empty. There's a strange smell, and I realise it's the volcano. In spite of the pervading dark here, strangely I can see the lights of Kos strung out in the distance, as if someone left the Christmas fairy lights on, and the red flashes marking its airport runway, close and yet a world away. The night is cold and windy, so it is wonderful to see the taverna illuminated within and the key in the door.

What a taverna it is! Perhaps the narrowest, cosiest restaurant dining area in Europe – there isn't space for two tables side by side. There's one table by the door, and another in the back. In summer they set up outside, but for winter nights this is enough. Yiannis invites me to sit in the back by the door to the kitchen, while Lisa makes herself at home on the stairs. Within half an hour, there are four customers (including me) and the taverna in the semi-deserted village is packed.

Sitting by the door, Stella and Costas have driven from Nikia, which has no taverna in the winter. They have brought fresh fish to be cooked, and order mezes and tsipouro, or raki – the strong, clear, pure liquor made from grape must, kept in big bottles in the fridge. Stella is a handsome Athenian woman who has lived on the island for twenty years; she has a shop in Mandraki and is also an artist. Costas is a Greek American, and I can hear he's not entirely comfortable speaking the language of his forefathers. As we strike up a conversation, he confirms he only comes here for a few months at a time, though for longer and longer every year, as he has returned to restore his great-grandfather's property. He has a nice sense of humour, and I'm interested to meet an American descendant of people who left.

Costas tells me that when he was growing up in Astoria, New York, there were more Greeks living there than in Athens. And that his great-grandfather's property was something he had wanted from when he was a kid. 'I said to my parents: give my sister everything, I just want the house in Nisyros.' For an American, it takes an incomprehensible length of time to get anything done here – but he's taking pleasure from the old things he finds. He often hears cows passing by outside the house. I ask him about the bath-shaped structure I saw this evening, show him the photographs. He and Stella are certain it was a *kazani*, which translates literally as a cauldron, for making wine and distilling tsipouro.

'I still have my grandfather's in the house,' he says. When his grandfather was ninety-three, he was making tsipouro one day when he lost his balance and fell into the *kazani*. He couldn't get out of the deep bath and was drowning in booze. Thankfully someone helped him out. 'That's how I'm going to go, though,' Costas says. 'Well, if I make it to ninety-three.' We laugh and drink to our health.

'What would make someone from England come to live in a place like this?' he asks.

I joke and tell him it's snowing in England right now; then I tell him about loving the wild, nature on my doorstep, a life that allows me time to write.

'Sometimes it's hard to get what you need here though,' says Costas.

'It depends what you really need,' I say, and Stella agrees.

My ears prick up again when conversation turns to a deserted harbour. Costas has another good story. He was there with a friend, a local character, but when he was ready to leave, he couldn't find him anywhere. Then suddenly his friend emerged from the sea, naked, carrying three fish to cover his private parts. 'How did he catch them, that's what I was thinking...?'

In October 2017, on a sharply cold, blustery morning in Mandraki, an exuberant wind was rattling the wooden shutters of our rented apartment and the waves beat noisily on the walls below as my mother and I left with Lisa in the dark. We watched the sun rise out of the sea, then we took the bus to Nikia. The well-kept village was empty, just a couple of Albanian workers hauling bags of cement up the hill. We gave up on any hopes of breakfast and started down the narrow footpath into the caldera.

The sun had not yet made its way over the rim or penetrated its depths, so a soft grey light prevailed. The earth was bare and brown before the rains; the only colour came from a few pinkish-red autumn leaves on the *gramithia*, or turpentine trees. The steep hillsides were littered with colossal rocks, some of which seemed to have crashed through terrace walls as they fell, though more likely the walls had been built around them. There was no sign of anyone. As we descended further, the loose path revealed small yellow flowers poking up here and there out of the earth, purple heads of heather and the green and pink of spiky euphorbia.

I also saw pieces of flecked black obsidian. In Neolithic times, obsidian was mined from the offshore islet of Giali to make into cutting tools; once, it also had an agricultural community. The other half of Giali is composed of pumice, and today the quarrying and selling of pumice for building material is on such a scale that it has chipped away that side of the island, turning it to brilliant white.

As we neared the flat plain of the caldera, I noticed an old farmhouse built from the surrounding stones, braced by a massive boulder, blending into the land. Although it looked rudimentary, inside it had the classic hooped stone arches of the *spiladi* or cave-house; all the old houses of the island were built with arches to be strong against earth tremors. Recesses in the walls made a simple fireplace and cupboards; small gaps between stones were filled with earth. Outside was a well-crafted circular water cistern, a threshing circle and a hole in the ground opening into a storage tank, the rounded interior plastered smooth. Just below the house was a simpler building, presumably for animals. As we stepped away, we saw rows of field terraces. Someone had lived self-sufficiently here.

Because of the fertile volcanic soil, the caldera and the steep hills surrounding it have been terraced and farmed since ancient days, and at times have been extensively populated. A deserted hilltop settlement, Nyfios, shows evidence of Neolithic and Minoan life; down below, just above Mandraki is a fort, a *paleokastro*, with giant masonry dating to around 800BC; and nearby are ancient cemeteries where people were cremated with vessels of olive oil, wine, honey, figs and olives. According to the account of *Martoni's Pilgrimage* from 1394, there was then 'an abundance of fruit' on Nisyros, including great quantities of dried figs produced for export. But also, at various times in the island's history, its fields have been poisoned and destroyed by falling ash. The volcano has been the maker and breaker of fortunes, bringing waves of prosperity and ruin.

Further down, we found a handful of similar smallholdings in various states of decay. The olive trees looked as though they might have been coppiced – instead of one thick, twisted trunk there were bunches of slender ones – perhaps to produce fence poles or firewood. Suddenly the sunlight reached us, turning the leaves deep green, warming the land, creating sharp shadows. Horned cattle wandered the seemingly bare fields among the olive trees and holm oaks. We had a sense of being alone in the volcano – as if we were the only people not to have heeded the warnings.

Our solitude was first broken by a lone motorcyclist. Then a car appeared, and as we neared the main crater I was surprised to see people carrying supplies into the café. Soon there were eight or nine coaches parked nearby, day trippers from Kos streaming out of air-conditioned vehicles. Assuming each of the visitors paid the entrance fee, the volcano earned about a thousand euros that morning.

In summer, up to fifteen coaches of tourists of various nationalities arrive daily. Once, I overheard two women comparing this with a 'better' volcano experience on another tour in another country; funny, but sad. The man who set up a refreshments stall beside the craters a couple of decades ago could never have foreseen the scale of the business he has today. Now, instead of farming, people own coaches and cafés and sell pumice.

You can package the wild and sell it, but it may still turn around and bite. That day, sections of the surface, including all the fumaroles, had been roped off, and painted red rocks were arranged in order to measure any movement. Kos, thirteen kilometres away, had suffered severe earthquake damage that year. The rocks are caustic, they can burn, and there is still an active hydrothermal system underneath. Ancient mythology, explaining the phenomenon, said the god Poseidon crushed a giant under a rock here, and that his hot breath surges out from time to time.

A kilometre along the road from Mandraki are the municipal baths of Loutra, constructed between 1885 and 1912. These warehouse-sized buildings, beside a small marina, housed a luxurious resort with three hundred beds. People came here from Egypt and Asia Minor to bathe in the hot mineral waters.

A building that once held baths is now a shell, the vast interior mostly stripped bare to the dark grey stone and white mortar of its walls. Squares of sunlight from the empty windows illuminate its disintegration: the wooden first floor gone, a wooden staircase falling to nowhere, metal pipes rusted. A middle section between two of the deserted buildings is missing its roof and façade, revealing the torn-off remains of plastered and painted walls, electrical sockets and holes for wiring.

The final building still functions, in a rather down-at-heel, old-fashioned way, offering 'sodium chloride sulphurous natural curative baths'. Its curving and polished wooden staircase, worn tile floors and tall ceilings, wooden washstands and paintings of the founders all evoke a faded grandeur. A sign handwritten in felt-tip pen gives opening hours and price: 5 euros for a bath.

During my 2015 trip I met a seventy-three-year-old gentleman sitting outside. Originally from Kalymnos, he had lived in Australia for fifty years, and was visiting the baths for his health. As a young man, he had been sent by his father to Australia to bring his brother home, but instead he ended up staying there. When I asked if he'd returned to the Dodecanese often, he counted off the year of every trip over the decades.

At one end of the functioning building I found a brightly painted café, decorated with antiques and run by Dimitra who rented it from the council. She told me she had come from the city of Thessaloniki in northern Greece for a holiday and decided to stay, living in one of the abandoned rural cave-houses or *spiladi*.

The only other customer that day, an older man with a grey beard and a sailor's cap, eating octopus cooked in red wine, looked up. 'In the old days people made things. Now we only break them. We only know how to sell things.'

A little way along the coast, the White Beach Hotel, something of an anomaly on an island without big hotels, looks to have been unused for decades. From there, the road descends to Palli, where the Romans built baths and then Christians built Panagia Thermiani, a cave chapel devoted to Our Lady of the Hot Springs.

It's speculated that when the founder of Western medicine, Hippocrates, established his hospital or health spa on Kos in the fifth century BC, he established one at Palli too. What is certain is that in 1910, a doctor named Hippocrates Pantelidis made use of the hot springs and built another therapeutic spa resort on a grand scale, even bigger than Loutra. The elegant Pantelidis Baths, advertised widely, attracted shiploads of visitors from all over the Mediterranean. But Hippocrates died eighteen years after opening its doors, leaving it to fall into disrepair. Its buildings, featured on many old black-and-white photographs and clearly visible from passing boats, have stood lifeless for generations. In the 1980s, one of Pantelidis's descendants attempted to restore the baths, but someone tells me that other local people, jealous of his business plans, launched obstructive lawsuits.

I walked through the gates, which were rusted and fallen open, although faded signs warned: 'Entry Prohibited, Danger'. A complex of buildings of varying shapes and sizes revealed itself, all built of black stone and white mortar, with sandstone framing the windows and terracotta-tiled gabled roofs. The downstairs rows of windows were mostly bricked up, while several further storeys stared dark and empty out to sea. A central atrium had soaring arches; I saw the sparkling reflection of water but found only a shallow, brown pool where I thought I heard the plop of a frog taking refuge. There was a gentle twitter of birds nesting somewhere above. Walking outside across a green verge to the rocks on the seashore, I saw piles of sand waiting to be used one day.

There are rumours that another of Pantelidis's descendants intends to finish the restoration and reopen. For now, the building is another haunting reminder of a century of change. Is the skeleton of the vast spa the remainder of a failure – or is it a symbol of human striving in a harsh environment? Those volcanic eruptions at the end of the nineteenth century had damaged people's livelihood; earthquakes and tremors troubled them for years. The Turkish and Italian regimes were harsh at times. People saw their resources depleted and went in search of better opportunities.

On the hillside behind Pantelidis Baths, above Our Lady of the Hot Springs, I saw the ruins of black stone houses, and as I continued around the coast, the settlement dwindled to nothing. Layers of pumice in the cliffs at Cape Katsouni, walls of black and red scoria, then a road seemingly to nowhere curving around the island, alongside a long stretch of wild beach where turtles sometimes lay their eggs. Birds of prey soared over the tree-covered slopes. I swam and fell asleep on the empty beach until disturbed by a noise – goats dislodging the rocks while reaching for caper bushes.

Morning of day two in Emborio. Wind rattles the shutters. From the terrace, the views are hidden behind grey-tinged cloud, the ruined walls all around making me feel as though I'm living in an old, forgotten castle. The green fields are strewn with rocks, walls knocked down by the goats and cows and no longer repaired. The roof of the house next door is gone, revealing a large stone oven that hasn't been used for decades.

In winter, there's nowhere to go to drink coffee in the morning, nowhere for people to while away a couple of hours in company. I'm happy to go back to bed and drink coffee alone under the duvet, as the clouds blow over the edge of the earth.

When Lisa and I leave the house around ten, it's so windy I don't plan on going far. At the other end of the village I find an old church but its gates are locked, so I keep walking uphill as the sun comes out and the sky brightens to powder blue. We find ourselves high on a hillside of bright green grass and yellow euphorbia, where tiny shepherds' huts are built into the rock facing into the caldera. Peeking inside, I find that even these shelters have archways to brace them against seismic activity, and roofs of heavy slabs of stone.

I sit in a curve of rock that protects me from the wind. Looking down to the sea, I see white waves crash over a shallow point where the island curves towards Pantelidis Baths and the harbour at Palli, where some of the people from Emborio moved after the 1933 earthquake. A bird flies up and away. All I hear is the wind gusting around the rocks, and the faint noise of work being done on a house. Emborio sits astride the ridge just below; a field juts out into thin air where the caldera rim falls away. I'm mesmerised by the sturdy terraces built all the way down the sheer hillside to create a tight horseshoe or amphitheatre, every flat surface carpeted with thick green.

Clouds return and I feel the cold. I'm not much looking forward to scrambling back down in the strong winds. Lisa suggests an alternative route, keen on following a goat-scent away from the village. It's only mid-morning, though I've no water with me, no map… But I've wanted to walk this way for a long time, and it's hard to get lost. As we head down the terraces dotted by prickly bushes, I'm excited to find old cave shelters, and stone steps leading from one terrace down to the next. This land was clearly loved once, and I imagine how gorgeous it would be in soft, calm weather. There's also the occasional dead goat, a reminder of neglect, but uplifted by the surroundings I continue descending until the land levels out somewhat, and I find an old pathway marked by solid walls on either side. Lisa eagerly pulls on the lead, enjoying the cool, breezy day and her own discoveries. In the direction of the sea there's the inevitable rubbish dump and a quarry. But inland, an abandoned farmhouse sits in an idyllic hilltop meadow, with curved terraces flowing steeply all the way down the slopes to the narrow valley below.

Following the well-defined path paved with smooth old stones, I continue towards Evangelistria monastery, thinking I might find water. A few fields here are used for animals, fences reinforced with wooden pallets, doors, fishing nets. The monastery, built of brown and grey volcanic stone with a church and living areas grouped around a courtyard with two cisterns, is recently painted but uninhabited and the tap is dry. I decide to continue, and spot one of the heavy-duty plastic tanks farmers use for storing water. I hope they won't mind if I take a little for my dog – and a cautious slurp for myself. Then I wonder about walking down to Mandraki to buy water, since it's only a few more kilometres. I'm enjoying the adventure.

Further on, someone's fenced in their field using old wooden bannisters, still painted bright blue, wedged between trees. Someone else has stuck a beehive between tree branches. Why do I like these things – just because they are quirky? It's also the sense of people making the most of what little they have to get by. We veer from the road down the more direct, steeper old footpath. There are more farms, some chickens, lemon and orange trees, a sunken church in a field full of fig trees – and gradually there are people. At last, we're at the edge of Mandraki, and I say hello to an older woman struggling up the steps with her shopping. I'd offer to help if I had the energy. Finding a route through the narrow lanes, I stagger into a shop and buy water and chocolate. A customer gives me a strange glance. I must look somewhat bedraggled and feel uncomfortably warm after walking for hours, so continue to Hoklaki cove, with its smooth soot-black pebbles, to dive into the waves.

I carefully retrace my steps through the winding alleys of the village. I pass the same older woman; but this time, she is running down the steps in tears, calling, 'I'm coming, Maria!' The church bell is tolling for a death.

We return uphill to Evangelistria and have a choice of three paths. The first is the one we came on. Another goes up the mountain to the deserted settlement of Nyfios – not for today given that the damp clouds are closing in again. I take the middle way, signposted to 'Volcano'. A well-built trail leads me through a lush landscape of olives and big holm oaks. It's easy to follow, pretty with the occasional deep red poppy or pink cistus flower, with its crinkled tissue-paper petals, and brilliant yellow Bermuda buttercups. I stop to investigate a stone building with its water cistern. It starts to rain and I wonder about sheltering but don't want to get stuck if the rain worsens and night begins to fall.

It's just after this that the path disappears. One moment it's broad, firm and clear – the next minute there's nothing but a scree slope at a forty-five-degree angle. I try going back a little, thinking I must have missed a turning, but this yields nothing.

I think I'll find a way through the stream bed to the left, but it's overgrown and impassable. I try clambering up the rocky slope beyond it, but that seems worryingly dangerous and I have to scramble back again.

Baffled, I look back to the scree slope and wonder whether I might be able to discern the thin line of a path through the loose stones, though it could just as easily be just a goat track. Still, it's the only option. Maybe a rockslide covered the path.

I follow it very carefully in the wind and the rain, and eventually it does, in fact, turn back into a path. But I'd rather not do it again. As I continue down the hill, I think how strangely scary an experience that was.

Then I realise it's a metaphor. For years, you follow a steady, traditional path – it may be strenuous but you know the way. You spend your life building something. Then suddenly, it disappears – an earthquake or a volcanic eruption or a violent invasion changes everything. You think: *I love this place, but I don't want to die for it, or to build it all over again just to wait for the next earthquake. New York isn't so bad, I've heard…*

We reach the road at last, and spot three little pigs, speckled pink and black, wandering in the fields beside us; I pass men in a field, building something, but soon hear them down tools and leave. Although it's adding unnecessary kilometres to the day's unplanned hike, I walk to the craters just to see that white landscape tinged with pink and yellow, to smell the sulphur and see the steam rising from the vents in the earth. I finally have the caldera to myself, just me and my dog and the pigs.

Later, back in Emborio, showered and changed, I'm ravenous. I leave the house and the steps are slippery from the rain, my legs tired from eight hours of walking. I hold Lisa's lead with one hand and my phone-torch with the other. As we descend the narrow alley, it feels darker than last night – the streetlights are out. I call Yiannis to check he's got electricity. He is coming soon, he says – it's just the streetlights that have a problem. I wait in the cold in the middle of the dark village and realise, looking up, that I can see more stars than usual, and the Milky Way spread out in all its glory.

Yiannis's friend Nikos arrives to open up, and it's good to get inside. It doesn't take long for the heater to warm the cosy, narrow space, and I help myself to a beer. Yiannis arrives and gives me a cheery hello as he dashes into the kitchen. The door opens again shortly after and a man walks in carrying a plastic bag with some green vegetable or herb inside which he says will be good for soup. Another man wearing a fleece jacket comes in and joins him at his table. We have a full house again.

I order the heaped salad I've been thinking about all day, and the garlic dip with almonds that's a local speciality, and bite-sized pieces of pork in a spicy wine sauce with ribbons of onion – too much, but I gradually devour it all, with a couple of glasses of raki. Lisa breaks the ice with the strangers, wagging her tail and gazing at them with her big brown eyes. I tell them I'm here to research deserted places, ruins. 'You've come to the right place!' they say, grinning.

We talk a little and then the man in the fleece jacket takes me up the stairs, where there are more tables, to show me photographs of Emborio as it was in the 1950s. There are women in white headscarves, and men in flat caps; men standing outside the school wearing suits and garters and big moustaches twisted at the ends; men holding musical instruments. And in one of the photographs, the people are standing just outside here, in the 'square': a big crowd gathered for a celebration in 1950. The two-storey building behind them is one I photographed this morning, with just the remains of a wooden door and windows, and washed-out paint with a faded ice-cream sign. The man tells me that the *kamara* or archway over the alleyway had a house over the top of it then. As we turn to go back downstairs, I notice a hole in the wooden floorboards, looking down into the kitchen. 'Bullet,' he says.

His father is still in Emborio. Few old folks live in these villages now, though a man who's over a hundred lived at Avlaki until recently and used to row to other islands for fishing. I talk about the stone buildings and walls, how they have lasted. He says yes, stone walls packed with earth are more flexible; they don't break like concrete does. As we discuss why people left the island, the two men tell me about another factor that hadn't occurred to me: rain. The people built terraces and field enclosures and barns for their farms. Yet on an island with no natural springs, a few years without rain would have made a big difference to the sustainability of those farms. 'They built those walls so they could eat. But they didn't always eat.'

On my third winter morning in Emborio, I wake again to wind and mist, and take my time with coffee in the warm bed, ready to pack up. The sea seems calm enough for me to take the midday boat. Then I hear it's been cancelled because of bad weather in Rhodes. So I have another day here, and will take the big ferry late tonight.

As I stand outside the taverna to get a signal on my phone, I watch a little black cat sitting in a hole in the wall. Lisa sees it and growls, and it jumps away. Yiannis, appearing from the kitchen, points to the hole. 'Put your hand inside.' I feel warm steam. It's a geothermal *apiria*, or blowhole of the volcano. 'There's one in the taverna also. That's where the name comes from.' Steam escapes through vents all around the island. One of them emerges in a small, mossy cave at the edge of Emborio, a 'vein' of the volcano creating a natural sauna.

Yiannis is rushing to take food to his chickens and donkey so I don't want to bother him with questions. 'Perhaps you would like to speak with my mother?' he asks. And so, in a little while, we walk up the alley and enter through a low doorway to Anna's house.

Anna, dressed all in black – dress, tights, shoes and cardigan – sits watching an old black-and-white film on television in a small room with photographs covering the uneven, green-painted walls, under a low wooden ceiling. It's funny, I think, to live in such a tiny space in an empty village on a semi-deserted island, but then I suppose it's easier to keep warm. There's just space for a sofa and a table and a few chairs, with a doorway leading through to the kitchen, and a lace curtain covering the window. She insists I take some sweets from a glass bowl on the table, and Lisa finds a bone under a chair, left behind by the last canine guest.

At first Anna seems reticent, but we establish that I know some relatives of hers in Tilos, and I tell her I grew up in a village in the hills in England. She confirms there were once three thousand people living in Emborio, *palia*, 'in the old days' – a fairly broad term. It was a big trading centre, she said, for crops like wheat and figs. When the 1933 earthquake hit, destroying the castle and some of the houses, people were scared and many moved down to the coast.

'But you didn't?' I ask.

'There, what can you see? Nothing! Here you see everything – the volcano, the sea, the mountains, the fields… And several years ago, some doctors came and they said the best climate on the island was here in Emborio.'

Others moved to America – or to Australia, she says. But her family stayed.

'And you don't worry about being so close to the volcano?' I ask.

'We're not so close. Nikia's closer.'

I'm not sure the volcano would respect the distance of a couple of kilometres. 'And how is it, with so few people?'

'We've learned to like the quiet,' she says, quite contentedly. She seems to have no complaints.

That's until I ask whether she still has fields. She can't work the fields anymore because of her legs and her failing eyesight – but that's not what she grumbles about. It's the animals that run wild. *Adespota*. 'They destroy everything. You work hard to grow things and then the goats, the cows come and eat everything.' For about ten years it has been like that.

When I mention my walk to Evangelistria, Anna says the building on the hill was a cheesemaker's. They had plenty of goats but they looked after them, kept them herded so they could milk them. People also had lots of vines, she says, and I ask her about the wine vats in the abandoned houses. They'd make the wine in there, leave it for forty days and it was ready to drink.

It's hard to imagine what it must have been like here with hundreds, even thousands of people – the noise! I say so to Anna and she points out there was the noise of the animals too, carrying things through the village and ploughing the fields.

When I leave, she says she looks forward to my return. I open the front door to a bevy of cats. Across the alley is a courtyard looking out into the caldera.

Quite a few of the houses were painted in bright colours, I realise, as I look around at the faded stucco on the walls and fallen to the ground. It would have been a colourful village at one time. Now, many homes sport large signs detailing how much money was allocated by the European Union and other sources to restore them. These mandatory declarations of funding detract somewhat from the beauty but that money has enabled local families to restore their property, and gives young people a chance to make a living here. There's one of those signs on the house where I'm staying; I am contributing to the gentrification and touristification of Emborio by staying in it, but it means Yiannis and his siblings are able to live year-round in the village of their ancestors and run a fantastic taverna that's used by the locals.

Anna's told me how to find the castle, or where it used to be – it's been bought by someone from Athens and converted into a house. I think about how people need to be able to move; how people from here were able to go to the New World and rebuild their lives, and people from cities have come here for refuge. I ascend the white-painted steps and look down at the village snaking along the narrow ridge in front of me, a few red roofs, a palm tree, the land falling away in tiers of green. The sun comes out as I reach the bright white church with white stone steps spiralling up to the belfry. Suddenly all the colours sharpen to magnificence and I must go out walking again.

As I set off, I have just the place in mind.

Taking the road along the high caldera rim in the direction of Nikia, this time I notice something different. Spotting a little opening in the hillside, I investigate and find it opens up inside into a shelter, like a bunker, a hobbit-house. There are several – probably used by people when they stayed to work in the fields. Another has an outer wall of black porous rock, with a back room that's almost hidden, built against the bedrock and braced within by arches that are white, black and red, the colours of the island. The roots of trees reach down into it from the hillside above. I continue, walking into mist. It seems that the fields under the oak trees are white with frost, but it's an effect created by little pebbles of pumice.

The houses on the slopes below Nikia are different, the stone softer for carving; doorways have post-holes and arches. The descent towards the sea is peaceful, the land gently flattening out, clouds obscuring the views out to Tilos but the sun shining through a gap to gleam silver on the sea. I sometimes take the road, sometimes find my way along the stone footpath, passing abandoned farmhouses and wandering cows. It's misty and damp and there are clouds of white almond blossom. I hear a donkey braying, goat bells, the hum of bees. The rock gradually becomes grey then black and suddenly deep red.

And finally, I reach the small abandoned harbour. Steps lead to a cove of jagged and pocked black lava. A few once-genteel buildings of sombre dark grey and red stone now stand desolate around a small boat ramp. Somewhere in the waters below, hot springs bubble up. Sulphur was mined here during Turkish times, and at one point by an

Englishman named Mr Martin. Until 1950, this was the main harbour for Nikia. Rowing boats ferried goods from big ships to storehouses on the shore, then donkeys carried them up the paths, and in return brought down figs, almonds and acorns to ship elsewhere.

It is just as beautiful as I remember. When I first came, I was in a hurry and promised myself I'd return to find the hot spring. This place is strange, lonely, frozen in time like the black lava, the movement of bubbling hot rock trapped in its shapes, shiny and wet against white crashing waves. Lisa jumps in for a swim, and I can't resist either. I strip off and climb down the metal ladder into the water, though we must leave quickly as the pale winter light is fading. Once again, finding the hot spring will have to wait.